Bryan Green : Parson–Evangelist

To Win Green

without whose love, good-humoured patience and loyalty
Bryan's ministry would not have been possible

Bryan Green
Parson–Evangelist

Edited from his works by Canon Timothy Yates

With contributions from
Lord Coggan
Billy Graham
Peter Grothe

The Bryan Green Society Ltd

An original paperback
first published in 1994 by the Bryan Green Society
68 Southern Road, Thame, Oxfordshire OX9 2DZ

Registered Charity No 220486

British Library Cataloguing in Publication Data
A catalogue record for this book is available from the British Library

ISBN 0 9524625 0 8

Produced by Fern House, Haddenham, ELY, Cambs CB6 3XA
Film: Goodfellow & Egan Ltd, Cambridge
Printed by the St Edmundsbury Press

Contents

Editorial preface

Bryan Green died on 6 March 1993. He left behind an unfinished autobiographical manuscript which he intended to be a contribution towards the Church's understanding of evangelism in a decade devoted to evangelism. His friends have collaborated with his daughter Gill and his son Mark to publish this manuscript.

We are grateful to Professor Peter Grothe, who has supplied material about Bryan's visits to America; he made more than one hundred, and the account is illustrative of his ministry as an international evangelist which also took him to Australia and New Zealand, Canada, West Africa and South Africa, India and Sri Lanka.

We have included a chapter, as Bryan himself had intended and for which he had obtained permission, from his earlier work *The Practice of Evangelism* which originated as the Moorhouse Lectures delivered in St Paul's Cathedral, Melbourne, in 1951. Further additional items are a transcript of a television broadcast – a fine example of his flair as a Christian communicator with typically imaginative use of personal testimony built into the presentation – and some examples of his writings in popular magazines such as *Woman*. Put together, these differing approaches help to show why Bryan was one of the most gifted communicators of the Christian gospel of his generation; many people throughout the world are grateful for his supreme gift as a preacher, but he also contributed much to accessible, direct and arresting Christian journalism.

We are also deeply indebted to Canon Timothy Yates who, while retaining Bryan's own words as far as is possible, has edited the text; to Rodney Dale for his publishing expertise; to Roger Hall for his help in promoting sales of the book; to Paul Mindelsohn whose administrative skills have been invaluable; and to Gill Bell and Mark Green, Bryan's daughter and son, for their constant encouragement, hard work, and background research.

Finally, we want to thank both Lord Coggan and Dr Billy Graham for their personal prefaces. They describe Bryan both as a clergyman in the church of England and as an evangelist – a 'parson–evangelist'. This was Bryan's description of himself, for he attached considerable importance in his own practice of evangelism to ensuring that it was rooted in the local church and congregation. It was with him and from him that we gained our own understanding of Christian witness, ministry and mission when we were younger men serving at St Martin's-in-the-Bull Ring in Birmingham.

Hugo de Waal, Bishop of Thetford
Peter Hall, Bishop of Woolwich
Christopher Mayfield, Bishop of Manchester
Peter Vaughan, Bishop of Ramsbury

November 1994

Peter Vaughan, Bryan Green, Hugo de Waal, Peter Hall & Christopher Mayfield
at the consecration of Hugo de Waal as Bishop of Thetford 17 January 1992.

2

Foreword
by Lord Coggan

On any reckoning Bryan Green was an unusual man. You don't meet many of them in a lifetime. He was glad that God made us individuals, and in his own individuality he rejoiced – he would give free rein to those marks which made Bryan Green – well – Bryan Green! By God's good grace there would be, as years went by, a process of refining going on, but that did not mean a process of taming – God forbid! Bryan Green liked to surprise us, sometimes to shock us, often to shake us out of our indifference. His restless energy put us to shame.

He and I went to the same school (Merchant Taylors'), though he had left before I entered. He was to train at the London College of Divinity, the theological college of which, many years later, I was to be the Principal. We were to meet on and off briefly as the years went by, and I would follow his work by reading the circular letters which he sent out regularly to his friends and in which he set out the principles of his developing thought and work. Our two busy lives did not allow of frequent or lengthy meeting, but we knew we were trying to serve the same Lord, and that was our bond of union.

Those who are looking for an orderly biography in this book will be disappointed. In the section devoted to his autobiography, we are given dates and names. A skeleton life-story emerges (though even the skeleton is lively!) – Oxford, World War II, Birmingham, USA, and so on. But it is autobiography written with one main end in view – to help us, the readers, to get on with the job to which Bryan Green bent all his energies, namely, *evangelism*. You could call him many things – parish priest, university chaplain, lecturer, preacher – but if he had his choice he would, I believe, like to be remembered as *evangelist*, and in that he would be right.

By evangelism he did not mean necessarily *mass* evangelism,

3

though often in the course of his work thousands would come to hear him. He had a place for the mass approach. But to him evangelism was something which informed all his activities, including the regular round of parish work in which, after all, he spent a very large proportion of his ministry. He was always searching for new ways in which an intelligent approach to the presentation of God's unlimited love could become a reality in the experience of ordinary people. If this venture did not work, then so be it; he would look for another.

There are those who wish that the Church of England would have set him free from parish work and let him loose to be a full-time roving evangelist. I doubt whether they are right, and I am not sure that he would have wanted it. Down the long years of his work as Rector of Birmingham, he was able to take off three (separate) months every year for his evangelistic work beyond the boundaries of his parish. Away he would go, to other parts of Britain, to America, all over the place, and back he would come with new experiences to share and new ideas to which to give body. The fact that, for the major part of his time, he was rooted in the day-to-day, face-to-face, down-to-earth work of a tough parish meant that his preaching could never take off into an airy-fairy cloudland. It was firmly earthed. He could never become a 'professional' evangelist.

He has left a legacy. Not a great deal of writing. His epistles (like St Paul's) were 'written not with ink but with the Spirit of the living God, written not on stone tablets but on the pages of the human heart' (2 Corinthians 3:3). Those 'human hearts' are scattered all over the world – in my journeys in North America I still hear Bryan Green mentioned with gratitude and affection. There is one group of men who would be specially eager to bear their witness to their debt to Bryan Green, and that is the men whom he trained in the parishes, especially in North London and in Birmingham, as his curates. Several of them now occupy positions of leadership in the Church, and so Bryan 'being dead, yet speaks'.

The autobiographical part of this book was written as the decade devoted to evangelism was about to begin. It was with this in view that Bryan Green wrote these pages – he 'slanted' them towards the decade. The book will appear while still that decade has some time to run. I believe there are many lessons to be learnt by reading these pages with prayerful care. In that conviction I commend this book to clergy and laity alike.

Donald Coggan

1955: Bryan Green preaching to American University students.

Preface
by Dr Billy Graham

One day towards the end of 1948 I flew into New York to speak at a youth rally. The talk of New York just then was of a British clergyman in his late forties named Bryan Green who was conducting a mission which was actually filling the vast Cathedral of St John the Divine. And he came to my rally! I shall never forget the encouragement he gave me that Saturday night when he came to the youth rally to hear me preach. I was aged just thirty years old and not in the least well known. Later I was able to attend his mission in the cathedral.

This began a friendship. I appreciated this friendship through the years and his support for me and my ministry. When we held the Greater London Crusade at Harringay, London, the open support of a man of his prestige and position in England was invaluable as we made our way. And he had me preach at the official service of the British Industries Fair in the great city of Birmingham, where he was rector.

Bryan Green's mission in the New York Cathedral was, in my opinion, the first true mass evangelism after World War II. As he tells in this book, its great success was spontaneous, not contrived; it simply took off, just as my Los Angeles campaign of the following year took off on a scale and to an effect far beyond what might have been expected. But always in his missions, whatever the numbers listening, Bryan reached out to the individual, to bring him or her to Christ.

Bryan Green and I might differ in some points of biblical theology but I thank God for his dedication to the Lord, for his witness to Christ, and his dedication to evangelism, which are all well shown in this memorial book, sometimes in his own words, sometimes in those of others. Probably no foreign evangelist had more influence on America than Bryan Green in his time. I read that he made no fewer than one hundred and twenty preaching tours in the United States. And I'm amused that he found, in the earlier days before instant world television made all accents familiar, that his British accent was one of his great assets when speak-

1961: Dr Billy Graham and Canon Bryan Green in Birmingham.

ing to an American audience. Because I found that in Bryan's own country in early days my American accent was a tremendous help in getting the Gospel listened to by Britishers!

I thank God especially for several facets of Bryan Green's character and career, which give this book a great relevance for today.

First, his missions were church based. In his case they were nearly all sponsored by the Episcopal church. As a distinguished Anglican he had a special entry there. And as rector of his church in the center of Birmingham, as well as being a travelling evangelist, he knew that the nurture of converts depended on the local church, indeed that the local church is the true center of evangelism, wherever it takes place.

Next he had a special gift for reaching students and intellectuals and what he called 'sensible people'. He could deal with their intellectual doubts, he could react quickly to the questions and situations which arise when confronted by large bodies of students. He could hold their attention. Against what he called the 'wooliness' which he found too often in official university religion, he stood unashamedly and vigorously for the uniqueness of Christ. And he could be really hard on students who mocked Christianity but had never bothered to read up what Christianity means.

Then I loved and admired him for his emphasis on the Bible and on understanding its meaning. He preached from the Bible, and he never diluted the Bible's message, that we cannot reach God by our own efforts. He did not major on the little sins of his hearers but on the overriding sin of separation from God. This separation, as he would insist, is shown by the 'great gap between the way we are and the way we ought to behave, between the perfect example of Christ's life and what we see around us.'

Then he would preach the cross. With all his force and charm, and the affection for his hearers which was obvious, he would show how Christ closed the gap of separation by His death on the cross. He would say — and it's only too true — 'Too often, you Americans think that you can "achieve" God. Don't you understand, you cannot by your own works "achieve" God. We can never be deserving of God's love, no matter how hard we try. That is the concept of God's grace.'

He preached grace. And he preached for decision. He once said: 'Beware of letting slip this note of decisiveness, this belief in the definite nature of the passing from "not being a disciple" to "being a disciple"; from being "out of Christ," "away," "lost," to being "in Christ," "at home," "found."'

Bryan Green loved Christ with all his heart and soul and mind. Christ was the center of his life, the heart of his preaching. That is why this book is so relevant to America and will, I trust, have a wide circulation.

When we went to his own country for Mission England in 1985, Canon Green's support and encouragement was very helpful to us. He had been retired from his parish for fifteen years but was still conducting evangelistic missions, though well into his eighties. At that time he talked about his life and work to our magazine *Decision*. And he ended: 'As long as I'm given life, I'll preach'.

God gave him a very long life, and strength to preach almost to the end. And now heaven is richer.

Billy Graham

The evolution of a Parson–Evangelist

The next section comprises seven chapters of Bryan Green's auto-biography as follows:

1 – Actions can change ideas

Why should any lay person want to read the autobiography of a clergyman? Why indeed? It might well be said of the parson, as was once said of the bishop: 'He was so heavenly minded that he was no earthly use.' But wait – I am writing this autobiography because I think it may be of some earthly use as the churches engage in the Decade of Evangelism. Let me make it crystal clear why I am writing at all. It is not that I want an ego-trip; I am too lazy with the extra work involved to do it just for that. Nor am I writing for the sake of contemporaries who from time to time joined me in some of my activities; most of them, alas, have died.

Why then, am I writing this autobiography at my age? I believe that learning from history is something that is often forgotten and left undone. In the case of evangelism, I believe that some of the insights and discoveries made by those who have been active in evangelism, may still be useful today and may be suggestive to others as a way of approach. It is for this reason that my autobiography is not so much about myself and the ordinary details of a man's developing life but rather about my activities in trying to share the gospel. According to my friends I have always been a man of action. I have tried to learn by trying and failing, and then using that experience to give me insights for the future. I am not a man who has done his theology simply through books and in the study although, like all professional people, I have had to read books and have had to study. My learning has really been in the action of trying to share the gospel both inside the church and, more interestingly, outside it in many varying occasions and circumstances. I have always been willing to experiment; I was willing to take risks, and I suffered because of that. Anyone launching out into new initiatives, and with imaginative ideas, who is at the same time forthright and therefore provocative, is sure to get hurt. Some may respond; and some will undoubtedly either feel threatened or take a different view.

In this short opening chapter I want to set down the main conclusions that I have come to through the insights and discoveries of seventy years of active evangelism, largely within the Church of England and mostly within the Anglican Communion. These themes will constantly surface through the anecdotes and the experiences of the autobiography.

I give first place to my absolute conviction that real and worthwhile evangelism must be firmly based in the local church. Here are the grass roots of all the sharing of the gospel, for here are worshipping Christians who go out both to speak the gospel to their friends, if opportunity offers, and to live it within the secular world by service to society in their daily lives and in their social circles. In his last presidential address to the General Synod of the Church of England, the then Archbishop of Canterbury honoured me by referring to a letter I write yearly to my friends, including Dr Runcie. He quoted: 'I am more convinced than ever that real evangelism – the evangelism which counts – is the witness of individual Christians within the worshipping community, going outside into the world to share the gospel which enabled them to worship in the Spirit.' He continued: 'The Church of England has more potential for evangelism in its parishes than the impression given in the media ever allows. Hundreds of thousands of English people live out their Christian lives in and through the worship and fellowship of our local parish churches. It is that ordinary, parish-based way of being a Christian which the Church of England must affirm in this decade.' This is my own experience in all parts of the world where I have had the privilege of seeking to share the gospel.

Another conviction has gradually been forced upon my mind. It is the need for 'witness' as well as 'proclaiming' or 'preaching' or 'teaching'. At appropriate times and in appropriate ways there is something very convincing in a man or woman standing up at a meeting or sitting within a group and 'telling it as it is'. That is witness – and if it is witness to what the Spirit of the Lord Jesus Christ has done within someone's life it is very convincing.

I have also slowly come around to the idea that most people seem to need a 'moment of truth' when, in some public way, perhaps with a small group or in a large service or meeting, the person is able openly to acknowledge commitment to Jesus Christ as personal Saviour and Lord. Clearly, I am not thinking of something embarrassing or difficult, which tends to make the person self-conscious, but a natural and happy acknowledgement of a fact. I shall develop this point later.

The last idea that will run through this book is my growing understanding of the spiritual power which springs from within worship itself. I am not thinking of the form of worship, ceremonial or non-ceremonial, extempore or liturgical – I am thinking of genuine Christian worship, however it happens.

My experience tends to show that worship of any type must be carefully prepared. Conducting public prayers must be to help people to pray, not just the saying of prayers. The teaching must, I think, be done in many cases by a course of sermons or a series of addresses rather than by 'one-off sermons'. Dr P T Forsyth was surely right when he wrote: 'Christianity is not the religion of a book, although it is a book of religion. It is the religion of a gospel and a grace. Biblical preaching preaches the gospel and uses the Bible – it does not preach the Bible and use the gospel.' Today, this surely means that we must teach the gospel in all the various angles by which God's unconditional love impinges or wants to impinge on the life of His children in the world He has created. This teaching to those who come fairly regularly to church is, I am convinced, best done by a series of topical sermons. By topical I do not mean a kind of superficial topicality but rather topics which are meaningful to people in many places and at many times of their lives.

These and many other insights have come to me in the very activity of seeking to be both a parson in his own parish and a wandering evangelist sharing the gospel in many different situations in many countries.

My title 'Parson–Evangelist' is very apt. It will quickly be seen as my story unfolds that I was a rather pious young boy, religious and decent living, because that was the way it was around me. I was a complete believer in an 'infallible book'. I was willing to de-Christianise others who differed from me. Looking back, I can see that in earlier years I must have been very unattractive to other people. I find this now rather unattractive myself, except from what I learned unconsciously perhaps. Led by the Holy Spirit, I moved forward, not really by reflection but by action and discovery into a more questioning, a much freer, a more widely catholic – but still deeply evangelical – way of thinking, living and acting.

1917: Bryan Green (left) with his parents and sisters.

2 – Childhood and school

I must start at the beginning.

I was born into a Christian family. I can never be thankful enough for that. As far as I can remember, I was not a particularly religious young boy. I was not especially interested in having stories of Jesus read to me, or reading them later on for myself. I said my prayers as I was taught to do. I read my Bible every day for the same reason. From the earliest days, church-going was a habit. I want to make it clear that, although I was not very interested, I never resented these religious habits nor the church-going every Sunday. The reason, I think, was because my parents were real Christians and believed what they wanted me to understand and discover. My father never said to me: 'I'm going to golf, you go to church with your mother!' That is what children understand and resent. My father and mother were genuine and that rubbed off on me.

When I was about twelve an incident happened which, on reflection, I can see deeply and subconsciously – and not so subconsciously later on – shaped my attitude to winning people to faith in Jesus Christ.

Let me set the scene. It is one that is scarcely believable these days. We went as a family to Christ Church, Gipsy Hill. In those days it had a morning congregation of perhaps one thousand people and in the evening another one thousand. The two congregations were largely different. The morning were all 'upstairs'; the evening largely 'downstairs'. Canon Joynt, the vicar, had two or three curates at the time. He was a good trainer of colleagues. What was unbelievable was Canon Joynt himself. Every day from Monday to Friday from about half-past two until about half-past five you would see him walking around his parish dressed in a morning coat and a top hat. Can you imagine it? It does not happen these days and perhaps it is a good thing too. He visited house to house in his parish, although calling especially on those who belonged to his congregation. His curates were supposed to do fifty visits each week and each of them had to report on Monday morning about the visiting.

I am not sure that it is quite true to say 'a house-going parson makes a church-going people'. But I am prepared to argue, from that experience, that a great part of Canon Joynt's amazing evangelistic and pastoral ministry was due to that thorough and regular personal contact with his people. There were of course other aspects of the church life that were both very vital and living. There was good preaching, and good worship, backed by a good Sunday School.

Then the incident happened. I was coming back from my prep-school when, in the distance, I saw Canon Joynt approaching, top hat and all. I was rather shy and diffident at that time, and he was a very austere and forbidding-looking parson. I did not want to see him but what could I do? I looked frantically around to find a way of escape but there was none. I knew that when he saw me he would cross the road and talk to me, so I waited for the worst.

Across the road he came. 'Good afternoon, Bryan,' he said. Raising my cap I replied: 'Good afternoon, sir.' He had no small talk for a small boy about football and the like. He merely asked after my parents and then something more of the same sort. Finally, to my relief, he prepared to say goodbye.

Then suddenly, he gave me a slight punch in the stomach and said: 'How are you going on inside?' 'All right sir,' I replied. What else could I have said to a question like that? He passed on.

That incident was implanted deep in my memory. Ten years or so later, it came back to me and I realised that here was a man of God, who took the trouble to bother about a young boy's soul.

Once I realised this, that incident made a lasting impression on my ministry. I have always tried to be concerned about people and with their deep, spiritual relationships whenever I talk to them. I do not always ask questions, of course, nor am I wanting to pry. But I am concerned – at least I am concerned when I am saying my prayers properly; when I am alert to the spiritual call of the gospel of Christ. Alas, far too often in my life I have been slack, and careless, and lost this sense of keen interest in the spiritual welfare of my friends.

I wonder whether this incident has something to say to us all in the Decade of Evangelism. Can there be any real sharing of the gospel of Jesus Christ, unless it is by and through people who are deeply, inwardly concerned in a most loving and open fashion with the spiritual life of those among whom they live and whom they meet every day? This is very far removed from proselytising; quite removed from any idea of interference with people's private lives. It may be nothing more than a thought or perhaps even an unspoken prayer, but it is a deep concern for others, just as God must have a deep concern Himself for all His children, no matter what state they may be in their relationship to Him. Dr Billy Graham and 'Mission England' got it right when they set up hundreds of prayer groups and asked people as they met to pray, to pray by name definitely for three people, that they might come into new and deeper faith in Christ. If you pray for someone, that alerts the concern and keeps us on the ball, as it were.

Reflecting like this, I have discovered that this inner concern for people's spiritual life frees us from anxiety – that is, over-anxiety – as to what happens when we meet them, live with them and talk to them. We are freed from anxiety because we believe in God's unconditional grace. He loves them more than we do, so why should we be over-anxious? Concerned, yes, but not over-anxious, for that is the way of proselytising, manipulating and a dangerous kind of approach to evangelising.

There is another principle here of great importance. Many people, certainly in the USA and also in other parts of the world, have had some kind of background of scriptural teaching and understanding of the gospel – still true of quite a number of people here in England and Western Europe. As with myself and so with them, the dawning into conscious experience that God is accepting us in Christ is a gradual process. As He Himself said: 'The Kingdom of God is like seed growing in the field – first the seed, then the ear and then the full corn in the ear.' I am in no way denying the truth about a sudden conversion – not at all. But with the absolute nakedness of modern secularism, coming into living faith in God is hardly ever dramatic or sudden. Usually, there is a gradualness of approach through Christian friendship, through experience of life, through crises of life, through one thing and another until the moment comes when perhaps, although not felt emotionally at all, the seed is ready to germinate into the ear and the person begins to become alive to Christ. You can use the phrase, if you prefer, 'he realises his baptism'. I must say that I prefer this to 'becomes a committed Christian'. The latter phrase suggests my side of the action, where the former emphasises – I am sure rightly – God's side of the action. He draws us to Himself; He gives repentance; He gives faith; He brings life, conscious spiritual life, to that which is dormant and growing within the heart of the individual.

During the two or three years that followed I pursued a normal life for a schoolboy: plenty of games, working hard and fairly conscientiously at school because of my mother's training at home, reasonably good moral values again because of my upbringing, but nothing else much at the spiritual level that I was conscious of. At fifteen it was time for confirmation, my parents thought. So I was confirmed. I remember well Canon Joynt saying to me – on reflection I think too hastily and assuming too much – 'I need not ask you, Bryan, if you have accepted Christ the Saviour and Lord with your parents' background and the training they have given you.' That suited me as a question because I could palm it off at once with the answer: 'Oh, yes of course.' But it did not register deeply with me; so the question did not arouse anything consciously about my inner life. After that I went every other Sunday morning at eight o'clock to the Holy Communion, because that was what my vicar had suggested and what my parents encouraged.

Then, another incident deeply affected my individual relationship with God. It happened like this. It was during the First World War and an older friend of mine came back wounded from the front. He was an earnest, enthusiastic, although very conservative and puritanical Christian. He approached me and said:

'Bryan, I think it would be a good idea if you could gather some of your friends, with whom you play football and cricket, and let me speak to them for three of four nights running about religion.' I was not impressed with the idea and then I thought to myself: 'Well, Mother, like many of my friends' parents, won't let me out on week nights because of school homework. But she would for religion, I know.' So I said: 'Well, I might be interested.' My friend went on: 'Right-O! Try to get your friends to come along but perhaps you cannot manage that.' He touched my ego. I said: 'Of course I can. I am one of the gang leaders and if I want them to come we will all come together. You wait and see.' In the event, they thought much the same as I did, because their parents thought like mine and they were allowed out for a number of evenings running just for religion. The first night we presented my friend with some fifty boys to whom to speak. He was a dull speaker. At the end he asked us to kneel for a time of silence. He did this every night. It lasted for about five minutes. When, much later, I started preaching myself, I remembered this and have always ended my sermon with two to three minutes' silence in the pulpit before I move. Sometimes I make no suggestion during the silence but, if I do, it is always something like this: 'Now God can do His business with us,' or 'Be open and let God speak to you as He will deep within yourself.' Most often, not a word, just silence.

During the third night, on 1 November 1916, we had the silence and in that silence I was conscious, with no emotion as far as I can remember, that deep within myself I had never told Jesus Christ that I loved Him, wanted Him to take my life, wanted Him to become my Saviour and my Lord. So, I did just that in the silence.

So far, so good. Then, to my horror, I heard my friend say: 'I want every boy who has asked Christ to become his Saviour and Lord in the silence to make an open witness by saying out loud by himself the last verse of the hymn we have just been singing.' I was horrified, in fact really terrified; I was, as I have said, rather shy and diffident in those days. All the people around me were my friends, with whom I had fun or with whom I was at school. Then the thought came strikingly home to me: 'You did ask Christ to accept you, did you not?' To this I had to say within myself: 'Yes, indeed I did!' Then I thought to myself: 'I must say it out loud. But, if I am going to say it, I will say it right at the beginning and not come on the band wagon in a weak kind of way following other people's examples.' I am afraid that is just what I am really like. So, falteringly and exceedingly diffidently, I said out loud: 'I am trusting Thee, Lord Jesus, never let me fall; I am trusting Thee for ever and for all.' What a fool I felt. Then to my pleasure I heard my best friend, who was sitting at the back and not next to me, say out loud the same words. I remember thinking vividly: 'Good, there are two of us now; what a difference that will make.'

I cannot imagine why, for my friend did not enquire nor did he ask me any questions, but on the way home I felt impelled to tell him what had happened to me. It was no transformation, it was not emotional, nothing dramatic, nothing was greatly changed. Alas, to tell the truth, I have committed more – and worse – sins since then. But something did happen, which is why my favourite verse is Philippians 3.12: 'I press forward that I may lay hold of that for which Jesus Christ laid hold of me.' That night He did lay hold of me and He has kept hold ever since.

Here, it seems to me there is another point about which the Anglican Church might reflect as it seeks to evangelise. It was well put by Arthur Fielder in an article in the Church Times on 11 August 1989 entitled 'Life after Billy'. Mr Fielder wrote: 'The Synod's idea of evangelism seems to be limited to information about Christ. Admirable, but it is not enough. Nothing is said about the necessity for personal allegiance or for public witness. Unless we reflect very carefully upon this, we shall see very few conversions, very few new Christians brought into the fold. Let us again remind ourselves of Billy Graham's direct words: "I am going to ask you to say: 'I receive Jesus Christ into my heart.' Then, just get up and come. Make that commitment tonight publicly." Can this be done in our parishes, done without Graham's hubbub and build-up and ballyhoo? Can it be achieved within the ritual and sacramental and ceremonial lifestyle or our catholic and reformed church?' I believe it can. Many of us have been inclined to do it over the years, and we would agree with Arthur Fielder that when people are called to a public commitment in the right way, in an unembarrassing, low-key Anglican style, they are greatly helped by this public witness. It brings out what has been growing within them over the years, makes it alive and vivid, makes them aware and keen to share. I agree it ought to happen at confirmation and of course it does for many people, especially these days when we have so many adult confirmations; nevertheless, that is rather too institutional to meet the point that Arthur Fielder and I are trying to make here.

Arthur Fielder closed has article with these words, with which I wholeheartedly want to associate: 'for it is upon this decision and commitment theology that the success of the Decade of Evangelism must ultimately rest.' This is why my experience on 1 November 1916 is still relevant in the 1990s.

I shall come back several times to this point of public commitment to Christ because of its great importance to the whole idea of genuine spiritual mission.

What happened after my open commitment to Christ? I certainly was not spectacularly changed for, after all, I was already living a fairly decent life based on Christian standards. I certainly did not have any emotional, shattering experience. I just knew that I had offered myself to Christ and that He had taken me. Then, an extraordinary thing began to happen. I found I wanted to share this gospel of Christ with my friends. To put it simply, I wanted to win them to Christ. In this beginning to share I discovered two points. First, that one must pray for one's friends before one tries to approach them. So two or three of us, including my great friend who had come alive to Christ on 1 November with me, met together once a week for half an hour or so to pray for our friends by name. I can assure you – and I really mean this – there was nothing precious, pious or particularly religious in our praying. It was good straightforward badgering God to bring our friends to Himself and to win them by His love.

Secondly of course, we took action – and here we often went wrong. We were really enthusiastic. We pressed the gospel upon unwilling hearers. I remember once a football friend blasphemed at me, good and proper, for daring to suggest he needed a personal faith in Christ. That was all very good for us, I am sure. Yet I suppose it must have done some damage – although, somehow, I think not much. I remember this coming home to me just before I left school. There was a meeting – in those days we called them 'Squashes'. There, various people offered their witness to Jesus Christ to their friends who were not Christians, whom they had brought along with them. I offered mine. I remember it vividly – for a fine non-religious fellow sitting on the floor by me said: 'You have put me off. I don't like your enthusiasm. You are too pushing.' At the time I was hurt, but now I see how right he was. Nevertheless, in spite of all our mistakes and over-enthusiasm a number of our friends, with whom we played football and cricket, did really come into living faith in Jesus Christ through our witness; then they started regularly coming to weekly follow-up Bible classes on a Sunday afternoon. Many of them began to come to church as well. Today some of them are still standing as practising Christians.

There is a lesson here to be learned, I think, but I am not speaking against enthusiasm – even over-enthusiasm. If young people in their late teens and early twenties are not enthusiastic for something or other they will be terribly dull when they are forty. I would rather have over-enthusiastic Christians, narrow maybe, over-pushing perhaps, but nevertheless enthusiastic. Dare I say that I think, without being insulting or patronising, that later they will cool down? But we need this enthusiasm from those people at that age. I found this immeasurably helpful in my pastoral ministry when some of my young people got on a 'high for Christ' and really went fantastically enthusiastic. I have always welcomed this and supported them and tried never to say: 'You will cool down later.' How silly you can be if you take a patronising attitude to a young person who is very keen because of a new discovery.

The next two years at school were quite uneventful. Because my birthday was in January, I just missed being called up, with, a commission in the army in view because I had been a member of our school Officers' Training Corps for a number of years. I was not clear what I was going to do when I left school but, somewhere in the back of my mind, I thought that probably I would enter the Civil Service – which branch I had not thought about. To get to the university I had to win a scholarship, because my parents could not afford to send me otherwise. Then something happened which in the end altered the shape of my life. A few weeks before I actually sat for the scholarship at Oxford, a clergyman from India visited the school and spoke, as far as I remember, to the Sixth Form about India. Afterwards, as a prefect, I was asked by the headmaster to escort the visitor to the school gates to see him into a taxi. As we walked along together, he turned to me and said, after chatting about my life generally: 'What are you going to do when you leave school?' I told him about the Civil Service and added that I had to win a scholarship in order to get to a university. He suddenly became more interested and said out of the blue: 'Are you a Christian?' This took me by surprise but I answered quite naturally and openly: 'Yes, indeed I am.' Then he said: 'I would like to suggest that you go and see a friend of mine at London University. He knows a good deal about scholarship possibilities.' So in due course, having failed to get a scholarship to Oxford, I went along to see this friend. He told me about several scholarships and gave me the necessary papers and entrance forms. It was only then that I began to realise what had happened; if I won one of these scholarships, I would have to be a clergyman, because they were for a theological college. I won the scholarship and thus I entered St John's, Highbury linked with London University. The college later became St John's, Nottingham. Now I was on the path to becoming a clergyman within the Church of England.

I sometimes tell this story to illustrate that a vocation to the Christian ministry need not be some sudden spiritual crisis or hardly thought-out decision. It need not even be made for spiritual motives, as mine was not. I became a clergyman simply because I needed a scholarship to get me to university. Not that I thought of it in those callous and secular terms, but that is how it was in fact. But then that is how so much of my life has been. I am never very conscious of God's guidance in my life ahead of time. But afterwards, again and again, I can look back and say with gratitude: 'Thy hand, O God, has guided my life from day to day.'

Oxford days

3 – College and ordination

My five years at college were uneventful. It was the first time I had lived away from home and after the first two weeks I thoroughly enjoyed the experience. Everybody was very friendly and the average age was a little older than usual, because the people back from the War were in residence as undergraduates. I took a three-year course to pass my BD in London University and then went on for a further two years to read Honours as a separate exam. In the event I did not take the exam because I was badly advised about the subjects for which to read for Honours – Hebrew, Latin and Greek. I was really not interested in languages so, although I did the work, I did not take the exam.

While at college, I encountered two things which were to help me in my future work in evangelism, as well as in my work in a parish. In the first place I came up against Biblical criticism for the first time. I was brought up in a very conservative evangelical background with quite a literal view of the Bible. At first the new approach was something of a shock, although our lecturers were very good, especially in the New Testament. While themselves rather conservative in their views, they gave us a very fair presentation of up-to-date Biblical criticism. In this way we got acquainted with Biblical scholarship and, after a while, I moved towards accepting it for myself – some of it gradually but, nonetheless in the end, very definitely. Because I had a good conservative background in the college lectures, I did not ever become very radical; I merely moved to the normal central position, which I think most Biblical New Testament scholars now accept. Clearly this was a help later with my general ministry and teaching work.

The other thing that was interesting was the field work that the theological students were encouraged to do while at college. One way in particular was a help to me. Some of the lectures on preaching I did not find very useful; they were mostly about sermon construction, unimaginative and rather dull. We did go out, however, and preach ourselves, particularly in the summer in the parks where families gathered on Sunday afternoons. In those days cars were a rarity and therefore the crowds were large. We used to take our stand where the people passed by into and out of the parks. I soon realised that what really mattered was not what you said but whether you got people interested in listening to what you said. This was what 'communication' or preaching was really about – not sermon construction but communicating with the hearer. Very quickly I picked up the idea, in the phrase of Clive Jenkins, that able Trade Union Leader: 'I try to put a hook in the psyche of my audience in the first two or three sentences.' It was great fun trying to get an audience to listen, or rather to stop and listen, and then hold them when you got them, while offering them in ordinary human language the Christian gospel.

The other field work was very different. On reflection, I am not sure that I approve of it now; then it was quite exciting. In North London every Sunday evening, near the college there were quite a number – eight or nine – of massed children's services. When I say 'massed' I mean as many as four hundred children all aged between eight and fourteen; quite impossible for any experienced teacher to speak to that group in mass I should have guessed, and to ask students was impossible beyond all imagining. Nevertheless, it was a challenge and after a while some of us quite enjoyed it. We took diagrams and illustrations, told Bible stories dramatically and so forth, which held the children's attention while we talked of the Christian gospel.

Looking back, and examining this for an insight into evangelism, I am not so happy. It was certainly good for us – excellent training – but it would have been better with some expert guidance. It is *what* we taught that worries me. Of course some of us emphasised always the stories of Jesus Christ and God's love through Him. That was excellent but to my mind it was too pressurising, too manipulative; it appealed to the children to give their lives to Jesus Christ. We did this with sincerity but was it wise? I cannot quite be sure. I could not do it now, but then I really could with all my heart. After all not much damage was done and hopefully some good. Who can tell?

That is all I need to say about college. When I left, I went for my first curacy to New Malden near Wimbledon, an immense parish of 23,000 people with a parish church and two small mission churches, a vicar and two lay readers. That was all. The vicar was without a curate, because he was very particular as to who he had to help him. Why he chose me, you would have had to ask him, but he is now dead. It was a great challenge. In one way it was wonderful training for my vicar was a remarkable man, especially expert at leading prayers at Sunday worship and at other times. I learned from him everything I know about leading prayers, and helping people to pray in worship, and have tried since to pass it on to my colleagues. But otherwise, what training did I get? A quick staff meeting on Monday morning and then I did not see him again. We were together only on Sunday mornings, because as a rule I was out on my own on Sunday evenings, either at one of the mission churches or at the parish church if my vicar was visiting a mission church. So there was very little appraisal of my work, very little advice except (from behind the scenes) prayer and absolute backing by my vicar.

Because of the lack of staff, although the Sunday schools were very good, confirmation candidates had always lapsed badly. It was such a large parish that there were a great number of candidates over the years. But where were they now? Nobody knew. I came from college, where I led a Crusader Bible Class for boys. I was asked to lead one in New Malden. I did so for two Sundays and found it quite unsatisfactory. Discussing it with my vicar, we hit on a plan to throw it open to girls as well as boys. Unfortunately, the Crusader's Union threw me out at once; mixing the sexes was not allowed in those days. Nevertheless, as I tramped round from house to house knocking at doors asking young people between the ages of fourteen and eighteen to come to a Sunday afternoon meeting on Christianity, I received a remarkable response. Within six months I built up a regular attendance of two hundred and fifty of these boys and girls — about half of each sex. They came regularly. They listened magnificently, running the service themselves, then listening for half an hour while I taught them Christian philosophy and the Christian gospel. Many came alive to Christ and have stayed on as Christians throughout their lives. Quite a number entered the ministry; some did other kinds of full-time Christian work.

What did I learn about evangelism here? In the first place I learned that you must teach the gospel; but the teaching of the gospel did not mean at the same time not preaching for decision. Any real Christian truth properly taught holds within its very nature 'the challenge for decision'. That is what I learned and that is what I tried to practice. I learned to be definite, to be clear cut and not to bother about secondary matters.

The other think I learned was to act as you really believe. Let me explain by an interesting story. On the first Sunday afternoon, we re-launched the opening of the class. I went down early to the hall where we were meeting. As I expected about twenty self-conscious teenagers were gathering by the door, wondering whatever they were coming to and what was going to happen. I greeted them with pleasure and said how glad I was to see them and went on to say: 'You are early, why not come in now, there is no harm arriving before the others.' We went in and then I turned to them and said: 'You know, shortly, when we begin, I am going to talk about God; why not come with me into this back room here and let us first talk to God?' They did not know what I meant; so they followed me like sheep. When we got in, as we sat round the table, twenty of us, I said: 'We are going to talk to God. Of course we can talk to God, sitting, standing, kneeling, whatever we like; but because God is so great and big and we are so small I think it is better to kneel don't you?' They all knelt down. I said, 'Don't say a word,' not that they would have done in any case, 'I will do the talking to God and, if you like what I say to Him, you can say "Amen" out loud or quietly to yourself.' So I talked to God. They were short, simple prayers. I stopped at the end of each paragraph and after a bit I got some "Amens", so I thought we were getting on not too badly. After about ten minutes I said: 'Now we must go into the meeting. What about next Sunday? You must come again.' In a few weeks we had, believe it or not, some sixty or seventy young people coming to talk to God. After about three weeks I said: 'I have been doing all the talking to God out loud, haven't I? It is about time you took turns.' So they began to talk to God and learned to express, very simply, what they wanted to out loud, unashamedly, quite naturally in front of their friends. I believe here is something that really helps evangelism. Once we get people talking to God with their friends, and in front of their friends, then we are creating an atmosphere in which real evangelism can happen, because people have been freed from self-consciousness by being conscious of God and not of other people.

I think those were the two main things that came out of my four years' curacy in New Malden. Not very dramatic or exciting, but very real. There is just one other thing I want to mention and that is my ordination to the priesthood in 1924. Cyril Garbett, then Bishop of Southwark, later of Winchester and finally Archbishop of York, gathered us together before our priesting.

I remember him saying something like this: 'If you are convinced, having seen a little of the Church of England, thinking and praying about it all, that the Free Churches are more right in their authority and in their teaching than the Church of England, then you should not be priested; if, on the other hand, you say, after prayer, that you are convinced the Roman Catholic church is more right, more true, then you should not be priested. Otherwise, you can be honestly and truly priested as an Anglican within the Church of England.' This made a great impression on me. It showed that one could be comprehensive within the Church of England, yet quite definite and clearly defined in theological views and in ecclesiastical policy. For evangelism, this has meant for me that I must stand where I am and be counted, plain and open where my loyalties are; then, within that circle of loyalty, preach the gospel as best I can.

1926: Bryan and Winifred Green: a rare moment of relaxation.

4 – Scripture Union and Oxford Pastorate

I am now coming to a much more crucial period of my life where I was beginning to learn more about evangelism and develop in my evolution as a 'parson–evangelist'. It is a period I could entitle 'Working on the Staff of the Scripture Union' and then as 'the Henry Gibbon Chaplain of the Oxford Pastorate.' In parentheses let me say that, in those days, the Pastorate was not attached to St Aldate's; it was a separate entity, run by a committee and organised and controlled by the Henry Gibbon Chaplain.

I enjoyed being on the staff of the Scripture Union, especially as the invitation came to me out of the blue and without my applying for it. It was unexpected and, for that reason, rather exciting. It involved travelling all over the United Kingdom, taking meetings for children, talking about regular Bible reading through the Scripture Union, and taking missions for young people, as far as I liked to organise them. It was a very good experience although, without realising it, I was moving slightly away from parish work into the specialised activity of offering the gospel through organised missions for that purpose. The Scripture Union was at that time largely dominated by the Plymouth Brethren. It was therefore very narrow doctrinally, believed the literal Bible infallible – God's Word written – and very puritanical about ethics. There had to be no dancing, smoking, drinking, theatres, movies and the rest. I found this quite all right and worked myself within that general atmosphere of theological and ethical behaviour patterns. Without my realising it, other people felt I was different. This became rather clear at the seaside missions that I took as a staff member every July in Ireland and every August in England. We attracted big crowds of children and young people. My house parties of helpers were students from all the universities, and other friends. They were normal, ordinary, fun-loving Christians, perfectly sound about the Christian gospel but otherwise very varied in beliefs and practices. This brought, unknown to me, much criticism, and files built up at headquarters seeking my resignation as being unfit to be a staff member of the Scripture Union. Fortunately, I knew nothing about this at the time.

Then, in 1931 I was asked to be a speaker at the great Keswick Convention – the youngest speaker they had ever had. With fear and trembling my wife and I went to stay in the speaker's house. We both felt quite out of sympathy with the atmosphere there, but we managed to survive it. The Keswick speaking went down all right, although I was rather amateurish and not very good, I suspect. But something happened there which did shape my life. One afternoon I was out in a fast sports car with one of the older Keswick speakers, a married man, very wealthy with two boys at university. We were talking about 'worldliness'. As he talked about the world of movies, theatres, dancing and so on, it suddenly flashed on me: 'Is that what worldliness is? Surely,' I asked myself, 'is it not worldly to spend all this money on luxurious fast cars, go skiing in Switzerland each winter and dwell in luxurious homes and live as my friend does?' It dawned on me. 'Worldliness' was not the things that the people around me were saying were worldly. It was something quite different; it was giving way to self-indulgence, behaving just like the secular, unchristian world does towards God and other people, ignoring social ills, poverty, homelessness and so on. I began to see. As my understanding of the needs and calls of society and what worldliness really is, what it really means to take a gospel to the world, I began to think in a way which ever after shaped my approach to evangelism as well as to teaching in my parishes and congregations.

A paragraph ago, I mentioned my wife. Win and I were married in 1926. I am glad to say, as I write this paragraph, she is still alive, three and a half years younger than I am. This is not a place where I want to pay a tribute to all her qualities, but I do want to say two things which bear on evangelism. First of all, she gave us a Christian home of great integrity and perhaps the hallmark of her character is absolute selflessness. She gave herself to Christ and then to those whom she loves utterly and completely.

This has meant an enormous amount to me and has shown up my own superficiality and selfishness in contrast to her way of goodness. Also, through all that she taught me, something even deeper became clearer. Of course I believed through the story of the Prodigal Son that God was a God of Love – that God's grace was unconditional and that He accepted us, not because we deserve to be accepted, but sins and all, just as we are, out of love and nothing else. Then through love He tries to make us more like He wants us to be. This I knew from the Bible and of course I also knew it from my own experience of a Christian relationship with God in Christ. Nevertheless, it was seeing in my wife unconditional love in actual living action, accepting me and other people just as they were, that brought home to me the reality of this great heart and core of the Christian gospel. For this, I can never be thankful enough, because not only has it meant so much to me in my own life, married and outside, it has also enabled me to see the heart of evangelism and to concentrate in season and out of season with this great message – the same yesterday, today and forever, never changing, never boring, always fresh and always making whole.

At the end of 1931, just before I was asked to resign from the Scripture Union because of all the protests, I was invited to go to Oxford to become the Henry Gibbon Chaplain of the Oxford Pastorate. I jumped at this invitation. So we moved to Oxford, and what a happy three and a half years followed! From the point of view of religion it was an interesting time in Oxford just then. The Oxford groups – later to be called Moral Rearmament – were in full swing and getting many converts, among them some Anglican bishops and other leading clergymen, as well as many people of the wealthier sort and many undergraduates. The great emphasis was sharing one's sins with some other person 'down to the boots'. After this sharing, you made a complete surrender of yourself to God. For those with Christian backgrounds, this was a deep Christian experience and many of the results were very lasting. But for some people with deeper perception the movement was fundamentally subjective and not in a true theological sense objectively Christian. A leader with this point of view was Bishop

Chavasse, then Master of St Peter's Hall. It was through him that I was invited to join and lead the Pastorate. He thought that I could lead in a positive way a movement that was not against the Oxford groups but which was parallel and deeper in Christian theology. I went to one of their house parties with my wife to see for myself first hand what it was all about and I came to the same conclusion as Bishop Chavasse, though I made some good friends there including the founder Frank Buchman himself. I saw at once the value of witnessing and began to introduce that into the groups and circles of undergraduates which soon gathered around me and the Pastorate.

It seems unbelievable now to suggest that witness was something new, but indeed it was. In Christian Union circles, the idea was that you preached the gospel; you proclaimed. You did not let people ask questions in public and certainly did not let them give witness. The leaders found this idea of witness hard to take, but I soon found that, by using it properly, it could produce splendid results by offering the gospel in a simple, honest way, provided that the witness was simply 'to tell it as it is'. I also began to work alongside people from different churches and a number of Anglo–Catholic priests began to work with me as we took students away each September – some one hundred and fifty of them – to some town to preach the gospel in all the churches who joined in organising our visit.

The most famous visit was the first – Bournemouth, 1932, organised by Max Warren, then curate at St John's, Boscombe. Brilliantly planned, it gave us every opportunity. I had with me Miles Sargeant of Pusey House, and Harold Ellis and Father Blair from Mirfield, to mention just three Anglo–Catholic priests in our time. Trevor Huddleston (later archbishop) was one of the students on the team, for the members, like the leaders, were mixed Anglo–Catholics and Evangelicals. This created quite a stir and enabled us to reach many churches and people whom otherwise we should not have been able to reach with the gospel of Christ. It also brought opposition. A very wealthy lady had promised £10,000 to the Oxford Pastorate – a large sum in those days and the money was needed. When she heard that we had been mixing with Anglo–Catholics, she withdrew her gift. At the time, I was heartbroken; then I began to realise that that is how it has to be. Take a stand on principle and you will suffer – but you must suffer gladly, if the principle is one for which you must fight.

There is an interesting statement in D W Bebbington's *Evangelicalism in Modern Britain* (p 251): 'A second, centrist school tried to minimise the divide that had opened in the 1920s between liberals and conservatives. Typically, like Max Warren, General Secretary of the Church Missionary Society from 1942 to 1963, the centrists wished to hyphenate no word like "liberal" or "conservative" with Evangelical. In the Church of England, it was also the position of men such as Bryan Green, who was prepared to ignore differences of opinion with other Christians in his zeal for evangelism, and Bishop Christopher Chavasse, who wished to hold Evangelicals together for the defence of Protestantism.' To my mind Dr Bebbington has not described very adequately the turmoil of the 1930s. There was much argument and discussion between the liberals and conservatives within the evangelical ranks at that time, a bitter division and calling each other by names, unsound or fundamentalist. I was black-listed as a speaker by the headquarters of the Christian Unions – the IVF; I was not sound enough to preach in certain churches, and so on. It was to be expected, because those of us who were in the centrist position (attempting to keep the gospel central and to minimise the divisions, especially with other Christians and other churchmanship within the Church of England) were in a battleground, often caught between two fires. We had to stand up and be counted, without being too provocative ourselves; at least I had to, because by 1931, without realising it, I had moved theologically into a central position, fiercely evangelical but unconsciously becoming more catholic and open.

At the time I did not realise what that was doing for me in my evangelising. It was of course making a vital difference, which other people felt, although I did not realise it myself. As I was more open, so I was more approachable by people right outside any Christian conviction or faith. They were able to talk to me, ask me questions and not have ready-made answers thrust down their throats. I was much more open than some others as I offered the gospel, not less definite but more tentative in my putting it before someone. After all, I began to see it was their choice; it was not for me to try to manipulate them.

I have already mentioned my use of 'witnesses' in teaching and preaching work. I soon learned an important point about witness. People who offer to give their witness must not be coached in any sense that alters their wording or the content from what they really want to say. Obviously, they can have hints about speaking up and so on, but no more than that. The art of witness is to get up and to speak quite briefly and firmly, 'telling it as it is'.

Let me give an example to illustrate what I mean. At one church we were having witnesses, four each night for five nights. I asked for volunteers, suggesting that those who loved Jesus and wanted others to love Him too might like to offer. I got my volunteers. I told them I would not coach them; they would just come and meet beforehand on the date appointed for each of them, pray together and then go and give their witness. As the volunteers filed out the vicar said to me: 'Bryan, you can't let that person witness' and pointed to a rather ungainly lady walking out, in rather unfashionable clothes. I said: 'Why not? She has volunteered.' 'But, Bryan, you can't let her, she has been in a mental hospital locally here a number of times and many people know this. She is well known in the market town too. She serves petrol at the central filling station.' I replied: 'She has offered, so she shall.' The day came. She had never spoken in public before. She came and joined me in the pulpit at the right moment. Looking around she said quite diffidently but very clearly: 'Many of you know me, because I sell petrol at the central filling station. Some of you know I have been in a mental hospital three times. I could never have been through all that I have been through but for the friendship of Jesus Christ. That is why I am a Christian.' She sat down. Convincing, dramatic, to the point. By a strange coincidence – or was it a coincidence? – the next speaker was a civil servant, very precise and typically bureaucratic. He got up and looked around diffidently too and said: 'Why am I a Christian? A very difficult question. I am not sure why. I think I have always loved Jesus for I was brought up by my parents to love Him. I have always been to church; I have been confirmed; I am a regular communicant. Yes, I think I have always loved Jesus, not properly but I have tried to love Him and that is why I am a Christian.' He sat down. Believe it or not, that was equally powerful. Not dramatic, very simple, ordinary but he told it as it really was. That is what counted and that is what true witness always is and does.

Before I finish this chapter I want to go back to an experience I had at a house party of the Oxford Group, where that praying with somebody gives you insight into the other person, even if you are not seeking at that particular time to discover anything. It happened like this. I was at the house party to discover what my attitude should be to 'The Oxford Groups', later 'Moral Rearmament'. I tried to be fair-minded and keep my thoughts open, so as not to be prejudiced one way or the other. This was especially important, because I had come to Oxford not to oppose them but, in a positive way, to start something different but equally effective in evangelism amongst students. I felt, therefore, at the end of the party that before I left I ought to talk face to face with the leader, Frank Buchman, with whom I had set up a pleasant friendship. So I said to him after breakfast one morning: 'Frank, I know you are very busy with many things during this house party but I will be in such and such a room any time between two and five this afternoon reading a book and waiting to see you, because I do want to talk to you for a little while before I leave tomorrow.' Frank agreed. At two o'clock I went to the room and waited there until about four o'clock, when Frank appeared. 'Where have you been this afternoon?' he asked. 'I have been waiting for you.' 'Come off it, Frank,' I replied, 'You always try to put people in the wrong if you can, so as to get a moral advantage over them. But not this time with me. I said I would be here between two and five and you could choose the time.' That silenced him. He sat down and said: 'Well, what shall we do now?' I said: 'Well, I want to raise some difficulties I have with your theological approach in this movement. For instance, this morning we had a lecture in full session about the cross of Christ by Eleanor Ford.'

'Yes,' Frank said, 'I know, and she talked well about the cross.' 'Frank,' I said, 'You were not there. I was looking around to see whether you were. I made a note. Eleanor talked for a whole hour about herself, how she died to self, or said she did, and said nothing at all about how Christ died for our sins.' 'Oh well,' Frank said, 'no good our discussing, it seems to me. What shall we do?' Instinctively I said, for no reason in particular: 'Let's pray together.' So we both settled ourselves as we sat to pray. Suddenly, Frank said to me: 'Get out a bit of paper and pencil to write things down.' 'But Frank,' I said, 'I do not do that when I pray. I just think of God holding myself in His love and as thoughts come to me about Him or from Him I try to talk with Him.' 'Oh well, as you will!' replied Frank, rather irritably. So again we composed ourselves to pray. Then I began to pray out loud. I forget what I prayed about; it was a very simple prayer holding ourselves before God's love, rejoicing that Christ died for our sins and that God loves us enough with his unconditional love to accept us as we are and so on. I am sure it was a thanksgiving prayer as far as I can remember now. When I stopped praying, there was silence for a moment or two; and then, to my amazement, Frank began to pray. I have never heard anything quite like it. It was a bumbling, mumbling, pointless prayer, saying nothing in particular to God or before God. He seemed really to be almost speechless and unable to pray. Then there was a silence before we said goodbye to each other. Reflecting on this afterwards I saw suddenly, as I have never seen it before, that when two people pray together they reveal themselves to each other. In that moment Frank had revealed to me that much of his religion was subjective; somehow or other he had lost his way and wandered from the Cross to which years before, at the Keswick Convention, as they sang that well known hymn 'When I survey the wondrous Cross on which the Prince of Glory died', he himself had come into a living experience of Christ. I felt sad.

From this I learned a number of principles. The first and most important was not to try and manipulate or try to alter a person's witness before they give it. It is so easy to make it sound more churchy, more theologically correct, or to 'clericalise' it and fail to make it the authentic witness it ought to be. The second thing I learned was not to ask people to be a witness too often. It is very easy for the witness to become a stereotyped affair. There is no reason of course why people should not repeat their witness on different occasions in different places, but not too often. I think they must bear the witness, 'telling it as it is', as it comes to them. I think this is rather different from sharing one's experience. It need not always be a sharing experience or a spiritual experience, although that of course is witness. But it can be a simple witness about why one is a Christian, what difference it makes being a Christian and so on. Witness should be more objective than just a subjective sharing, a difficult balance to try to achieve. This is important, if witness is to be effective and not off-putting, helping other people to see the value of living faith in Jesus Christ.

Another fact became very clear to me as I was working among students in Oxford in the 1930s. It is very easy to sneer at what is called 'Public School religion'. Of course there was compulsory chapel, of course it was rather conventional, and of course by healthy teenagers it was sometimes resented and turned them away from, rather than towards Christianity. Nevertheless, they learned something about the Christian facts and the Christian story. This was why many of them, when they came up to the university, were ready to come alive to that which they had known in their minds and perhaps had even resented; to come alive to it in a real and committed way. It is not the least surprising that a great number of Christian conversions, and commitments to Jesus Christ, happen during university years. Life is being faced in a different way and one has to stand on one's own feet. Perhaps it is then that the power of Christ can come home meaningfully to a young person. At any rate, I learned not to sneer at Public School religion. Moreover I learned also not to sneer at the religious education given in our State schools, especially our Grammar schools. It was Christian knowledge anyhow and we were not dealing in those days in Oxford with utter pagans. Most of the young men and women who were students then had some knowledge of Christian faith and the Christian story. You could speak to something. It was not to a mind blank about the Christian gospel. That is why it was a good opportunity for evangelism. One must not belittle what people have, but build on it and base one's appeal upon it. This is certainly a lesson I learned while working among students in those days in Oxford.

Then came an incident which also shaped my ministry very markedly. I mentioned before that Cyril Garbett, then Bishop of Winchester, had always looked after the young men whom he had ordained. I was no exception, so when I heard he was coming to Oxford on some business matter or other, I wrote to him and asked if he would spare a little time to see me, as I wanted his advice. He replied promptly and I went to see him. The matter I wanted to put before him was simply this. In September, two months before, I had been approached by the Bishop of London and invited to become vicar of Christ Church, Crouch End. This was an interesting parish of educated people near Highgate in North London. The Bishop did not press me for an answer but I knew that, about the time when the Bishop of Winchester came up to Oxford, I had to make a decision. He listened very carefully to what I had to say and then said: 'Bryan, here is my advice. You must make a decision. It is your responsibility. If you wish to continue in a specialised ministry, among students, where you are very successful, then don't accept this invitation. But if, on the other hand, after careful reflection and prayer you decide that your real ministry is among ordinary people in an ordinary parish within the Church of England, in quite an ordinary parochial way, then accept this invitation. For if you do not become a parish priest now and learn to make your mistakes early on and learn by experience, then you will not be ready for higher responsibility in the parochial sphere later on.' I thanked him for his advice and promised to consider it.

Later on that week I was down in the West End of London leading a Bible study group. Something happened to me as it very rarely does. As I was giving the Bible reading, I had a clear, inner conviction out of the blue (because I was not thinking about it then consciously) that I had to say 'yes' to this invitation. So, as soon as I returned to Oxford, I wrote a letter to the Bishop of London to say that I would count it a privilege to become vicar of Christ Church, Crouch End.

5 – Into parish ministry:
Crouch End and Holy Trinity, Brompton

I had no wish to leave Oxford. The work among the students was going very well. Nobody wanted me to leave. They all wished me to stay but I knew I was going to move on. But as I moved on I began to realise I was a different person from the young clergyman who had come to Oxford three and a half years earlier. I no longer accepted the literalness of the Bible, though I kept the Bible as the Word of God and my final authority. No longer was I bound by puritanical ethics. I was quite prepared to live in the world in a normal, ordinary life bearing what Christian witness I could. No longer did I believe that one can only preach the gospel a certain way; nor did I think it was wise to press people and manipulate them in evangelism. Without knowing it, quietly and unconsciously during the three and a half years, religious life at Oxford and my experience with students had moulded me into a more liberal, outward-going, listening pattern of person and of ministry. I cannot be thankful enough for what Oxford and my many friends there and members of the university gave to me during those years. I may have helped many but certainly I was helped myself.

So I came to Crouch End and plunged into my first experience of being a vicar in a parish.

In one way it was easy; in other ways it was very difficult. It was easy because, for reasons of leadership, the congregation had shrunk and shrunk and shrunk. The normal congregation was about two hundred on Sunday morning and only about one hundred and fifty on Sunday evening. The fact that the church held together at all was due to four or five families of devoted Christian church-goers, each with a number of teenagers who still loyally supported the church. Also helping to keep the church together was a brilliant organist – temperamental, like all great

43

organists are – director, among other things, of the Alexandra Children's Choir for the BBC, so he was very well known. He was also a composer of church music. Dr Walker-Robson was certainly a personality, and not an easy one, and I was told that I must get along with him. I was plunged into this situation to face it as best as I could. Fortunately, the families gave me loyal support even without knowing me, for they had wanted a young vicar. As we got to know each other, their support developed into real friendship and I had unlimited backing for all I tried to do. 'Robbie' Walker-Robson was an interesting problem. My first reaction was to tell him frankly that I was not musical. This honesty I always found to be valuable. When I said: 'You must show me how to manage the services. I will leave the musical side to you; but teach me to appreciate music, so when your choir sing beautiful anthems, I can worship as I listen to them.' Then I added: 'Come and pray with me on Sunday morning for ten minutes before we go into church.' Very quickly Robbie and I became close friends and real collaborators. This kind of friendship and collaboration, I believe, was the basis for a true parish ministry. With the preaching of the gospel, and good music and singing, the congregation began to grow. It was not long before we had six hundred (the church capacity) in the evening, often with chairs in the aisles, and about five hundred in the morning. Then I began to understand something more. It is not sufficient simply to offer the gospel, that people may come to accept Christ as Lord and Saviour. I must lead them on in the Christian life. But how? This was a new experience for me in a parish setting. I had the idea of a Thursday training fellowship; everybody who came had to commit themselves to attend regularly. We learned about the gospel, we talked about sharing it, passing it on to our friends, bringing them to church, helping them to faith and about all matters concerned with evangelism. Looking back, I can see now that I was beginning to understand that people will only grow in the Christian life if they are trying to share what they have with those with whom they come into contact. This is a reflection which I think is of importance in the Decade of Evangelism or for that matter at any time in the history of the Christian church. There is nothing new in it. It is New Testament teaching. The first disciples went out and passed on what they had discovered. That is exactly what I was training my people to do. Some did and some did not.

But here I soon discovered an important point to remember for all those who work within the ambit of the ordinary Anglican parish. There are some very good Christians who temperamentally are not suited to articulate the gospel in words. They articulate the gospel of God's love best in their lives and by the service of their hands and feet, but not by words. I remember one of our very best, middle-aged Christians, Eileen Blake, coming to me in great distress. She had been to some meeting outside the parish – I forget which one it was – where she had been told and taught that if you want to be a proper kind of Christian you must talk about Jesus Christ to your friends. She was to put into words what she wanted them to believe and understand what she had discovered. She told me that she could not do that, as she was not any good at speaking. I replied: 'Eileen, I am so glad you see this. You would make such a mess of speaking if you know it does not suit you.' She beamed at me in pleased surprise, grateful to be released. I said that she was not that kind but another kind of Christian. I knew her well enough to know the way she was living it in her life. I knew the wonderful Christian service she was giving. I knew all these things: her way of passing on the gospel of Christ, by life and not by word. It is most important to release any of our people from the guilt of not speaking when, in fact, it is not cowardice or lack of something to say but, frankly, they are not articulate people about the things they feel deeply. Many people are not, and why should they be? God has His different children and has no favourites. He does not expect us all to be the same. This is good New Testament teaching about the differing gifts of the Spirit.

While I was in Crouch End I had the first opportunity of preaching the gospel on the radio for the BBC. I cannot be too grateful for this opportunity. In the first place, I found the training given by the BBC very good indeed. I thought at first that repeating my sermon several times over would spoil it. I discovered that is not true. After three or four repetitions you feel at ease with it, more at home with it, you can manoeuvre it or mould it to suit what you are trying to say. I also learned the importance of timing. In those days the BBC was very particular with a sermon; it had to be right on the mark and timed within thirty seconds. It was good discipline, I found, and it trained me in putting my thoughts concisely and simply. It also taught me to use simple words that ordinary people would understand, to which they would listen. I had to learn to interest the unseen listener and, as I spoke, to forget the microphone; or, rather, imagine the microphone was the person in my own home, to whom I was speaking face to face. It was excellent training for evangelism and that is why I was glad to have the privilege of broadcasting quite often. Of course there is a value in the broadcasting itself, which reaches a great number of people, but I am now thinking of the value to the broadcaster, training him to be an effective communicator of the gospel.

In 1936 another interesting event occurred in my life. Out of the blue, I was asked by the chaplains at Cambridge University to be the Anglican leader in the triennial mission for the university. The previous leader had been Archbishop William Temple. I accepted the invitation. Looking back now I wonder how I had the temerity to do this. But I was pressed by Professor Raven and others, who wanted me to do it. So I felt impelled to say 'yes'. My assistant missioner, who took the pastoral addresses in the earlier afternoon or lunchtime, was Canon Peter Green, the famous Anglo–Catholic evangelist, then Rector of Salford. He was a remarkable man, a great evangelist and a marvellous parish priest. Rumour has it that he refused four diocesan bishoprics – I think this was true. The Free Church people had as their leading missioner Dr John Whale and as assistant missioner the Reverend Leslie Weatherhead. We certainly were an interesting team. To my amazement, the students turned out in great numbers to hear all of us, in my case filling Great St Mary's with two thousand students every night for eight nights. I had never faced anything like this before in my life. I offered the gospel in a teaching fashion night after night. Canon Peter Green confided to me afterwards that he could not understand what I was doing; I seemed to make no appeal for commitment, but just stated the gospel and offered it, hopefully making the truth sound sensible. He then said to me:

'But, Bryan, I understood when Thursday night came: you made the appeal and asked people who wanted to commit themselves to Christ, or had committed themselves to Christ during the previous nights, to stay behind in the side chapel, to make an open commitment to Christ and so that you might pray with them.' It was a valuable way of handling things – not every night, but when you believed the gospel had done something in the minds and hearts of some of the listeners.

At the time this was a very kind remark but on reflection I can see that there was something here that was really important, upon which I had unconsciously stumbled. I agree that, if you follow the way I did, you miss people who perhaps only come one or two nights before the moment of the appeal occurs. That is true. On the other hand the gain is immense. You are not pushing people, not hurrying people. You are making people realise, by the very fact that you expect them to come willingly, that becoming a committed Christian is not necessarily an easy matter. It takes a serious outlook and a serious effort, with the spending of time and thought, before you can make a proper commitment to God in Christ. So, on the whole, I think this is also the right way of approach in a parish, where it is easier, because you have people coming Sunday after Sunday. Even before they call themselves committed Christians they still come, which is a good way of drawing people towards our Lord.

I was very happy at Christ Church, Crouch End during the three and a half years I was there. It came as quite a surprise, not an altogether pleasant one, when in September 1938 I received an invitation from the Bishop of London to leave Crouch End and move down into the West End to become vicar of Holy Trinity, Brompton. I tried to find out how the invitation came. I discovered that a group of laymen in the church there had enjoyed the way in which I had taken the three-hour Good Friday service. Having made enquiries, I felt I must accept the challenge of this invitation. So, in the early autumn, Win and I moved down from North London to the vicarage in Brompton Square. At that time, the congregation at Holy Trinity was a large one, with about a thousand people, even filling part of the galleries as well as downstairs, every Sunday morning. They were upper-middle-class people, some members of the aristocracy, very intelligent, some were young, though most were middle-aged and older. They were very loyal and regular church-goers and willing to support a straightforward teaching ministry. Naturally they hated change, but were not narrow minded. I was only thirty-seven; in retrospect, I think I was too young to become a vicar of that kind of affluent West End congregation. But there it was. I had accepted.

Unfortunately, I could not have come on a worse Sunday, from my point of view, as a new vicar. On 29 September that year Neville Chamberlain had come back from Munich, waving his umbrella and proclaiming 'peace with honour'. The very next Sunday was my first. I was telephoned by one of the wardens who expressed the hope that amongst the hymns we could have 'Land of Hope and Glory' and the 'National Anthem'. I happily agreed to the National Anthem but did not say anything about the other. Of course, we did not have it! Sunday morning came and at 11.00am I went into church and found, as I had expected, that it was packed to the doors – standing room only – twelve hundred people. No doubt a few came to see what the new vicar was like, but most of them came full of great relief and rejoicing that the bombing had not happened and we were not at war. This indeed was understandable; I could sympathise, but what worried me was their attitude. They were so relieved that they had escaped through appeasement from the inconvenience, as well as the suffering, of a war.

The time came for the sermon. I can still remember it most vividly, so emotional was the effect it had upon me. I 'crawled up' into the pulpit. I started off, I remember, something like this: 'This is a bad Sunday for a new vicar to preach to his congregation for the first time. But I want to make clear to you straight away how I propose to preach to you as long as I am here. There are three things that I can do. I can preach the gospel of Christ by saying words of platitude. This, I hope I shall never do. I can preach the gospel, unrelated to the circumstances in which I am preaching it or to the people to whom I am preaching it: this, again, I hope I shall never do. Thirdly, I can preach the gospel to and through the situation in which we are, to the people who are present. This I shall always try to do and shall try to do now.' I went on: 'My text is this: "You are bought with a price"' and added: 'and the price is the sacrifice of Czechoslovakia.' I continued by saying that this was not a day of peace with honour; it was peace at any price, by means of appeasement of a bully and tyrant. Our nation should be filled with shame at the dishonour we have suffered in the eyes of the world. So I went on preaching along those lines. I could feel the hostility as I was preaching. You could have cut the atmosphere with a knife. There was no problem in getting them to listen. At the end of the service I went to the door to say goodbye. Many spoke strongly against what I had said. In fact, the wife of one of my Church Wardens was so worked up that she spat out her words of disapproval as she left and some of the spit landed on my face. Quite unintentional, I am sure, but it showed how angry she was. By that one sermon, I lost one hundred of my congregation. There were pew rents in those days, so it meant a financial loss, too, but that did not matter. Some of them came back but a number went to other churches, I hope. Did I regret what I had said? No, I was glad, but upset. On reflection, I became nothing but glad because I realised that, unconsciously to me, in His goodness God had helped me save my soul. As a young clergyman, I could easily have lost it in the affluence, intelligence and aristocratic surroundings in which my ministry was now cast for the time being. In the end, it did not harm me, because in three months' time the church was packed out every Sunday and the young people had increased by at least four-fold, lots of them men. I learned something then. You have got to stand up and be yourself, preach the gospel as you see it, fearlessly and clearly with conviction.

This was the first of a number of interesting things that happened to me during my ten years at Holy Trinity, Brompton.

The first twelve months were uneventful, except that Holy Trinity got a reputation for plain gospel teaching and very good music, with an excellent choir of boys and men. All seemed to be going well. About six months after I arrived there, I was invited by the Chapter of the Rural Deanery, consisting of about thirty clergymen, to speak to them on 'Conversion in a West End Parish'. I talked with them and explained, among other points, my belief that there needed to be a call for commitment, to decision for Christ, from time to time, however that call was made. I explained that, although many people came gradually into faith in Christ, for very many people there was a necessary kind of conscious crisis in one way or another. We had to preach remembering the need this presents to some people.

When I finished the discussion, I found to my dismay that I was alone in making this point amongst all those other fellow clergymen of mine in neighbouring parishes. I also made an interesting point, which again I found was disregarded. We had a great number of weddings in those days in my West End church. Holy Trinity was one of the foremost, with about eighty to a hundred weddings every year. I told them, although my experiences were only of short duration, that the best thing about pre-marriage interviews was that you could talk about spiritual things because people were alive at that moment to that sort of approach. I pointed out that the passage from the Bible which says 'He that loveth is born of God' means what it says. True love seems to produce within people a sense of 'the spiritual', which at other times of their life they do not recognise. I am talking now of course about real love, not just a sex motivation or a marriage for convenience or any other of the superficial reasons which sometimes bring people to church for weddings. If there is true love – and in most cases I found it to be true – the couple are open to a sympathetic and understanding talk about God and how His love was the love which they were reflecting in their love and how He wanted to enter consciously by their acceptance of His love into their lives and to share their love with them in the years ahead. As I made this point to my fellow clergymen, I found the response was disappointing. Instead of welcoming it and seeing my point, they merely said they would not have time to do those kinds of interviews and had too busy a life for that sort of discussion. Writing as I do now in the 1990s, this is almost unbelievable, because nowadays pre-marriage counselling is the common practice of most clergy; but it was not then. What I learned from their reaction was not, simply, that they could not find time for this most important matter, but that they did not see the opportunity of presenting the gospel of Christ to people who may be conventional church-goers but who are at a moment in their lives when they might be prepared to listen.

In September 1939 came the outbreak of war. Some of you may remember the first air-raid warning after war was declared – a declaration we first heard over the radio from Neville Chamberlain. It occurred at about 11.30 on Sunday morning. We had been listening to the declaration of war; we had a loudspeaker or two in church as a special announcement was expected. A short time later we heard the air-raid sirens going. Naturally, I stopped the service and said: 'That is an air-raid alarm. You had better go down into the crypt.' I can see those West End people now – stiff upper lips, showing not a trace of panic or fear – walking sedately out through the vestry and down the stairs. We had not been down below many minutes before the 'all clear' went. So, out we came and continued our service. But Holy Trinity was never the same again, because my normal congregation dwindled from over one thousand to about three hundred on Sunday morning in one fell swoop. Many of the people stayed in their country homes away from bombs and war – understandably and rightly at their age. Others were called up to military service or their businesses moved out of London.

To take their place we had to re-build the congregation. It was not too difficult really in the first year of the war. There were no bombs and people were flocking into London on military and other duties in the public service. So I was able to build it up and bring back the numbers to their pre-war size. I was helped in this, partly, by curtaining out the church at some expense, so that we could continue to have an evening service in spite of the 'black-out'; and also by the fact that my organist was able to stay with me and for the Sunday morning service we brought in our boys' choir by bus from the country whither the choir school had moved. The evening choir was a very special choir recruited largely from BBC singers and from London choirs which had disbanded. Some of them, especially the men, came to us also on Sunday morning, so the quality of our singing greatly improved.

The Blitz scattered the congregation again but not so badly as before; once more, I had to set to work to rebuild the congregation to its former strength. You may not believe it but this happened a third time when Flying Bombs started; again, I had to go to work to pull things round. I do not know that I learned very much from this except, perhaps, that it was important to plod on with teaching and preaching regardless, to do one's pastoral work no matter what was happening, to identify oneself with the people around.

As I was officiating chaplain to the Communication Control of the Anti-Aircraft Defence of London, whose headquarters were in my parish, I had to identify myself with these people – and I enjoyed it. I found the contact with the military, both men and women, most interesting. They came to the compulsory 'padre's hour' and, although I found them a little hesitant in asking questions and very reluctant in some cases to take part in a discussion, they seemed to listen to me and moderately enjoyed what I tried to say to them.

One incident occurred, which I found instructive both then and later, when I got to Birmingham. The colonel in charge of the unit made the Sunday morning service, an hour before our usual one, compulsory. At one point, in response to younger officers coming along, he agreed to take a vote of the soldiers as to whether the church service should be compulsory or not. To his surprise, and to their surprise, by an overwhelming majority they voted for a compulsory service. They made their reasons clear. They argued that, if it was voluntary, then to choose voluntarily to go to church would make out that you were better than your pals and you could stand out like a sore thumb. But if it is compulsory, as they put it, we can all grumble together and say that we do not want to be there and then settle down to enjoy it, while it is the kind of live and friendly service that a compulsory service can be. That said something about what people outside think.

I think there is no doubt about the value that we were able to turn the crypt – quite an extensive space under the church – into what we called the Dug Out, to act as a canteen for the men and women in the neighbourhood, especially those attached to the unit of which I was chaplain. We did this, I am glad to say, in co-operation with our very good friends, the members of the Church of Scotland at St Columba's, Pont Street. There was no doubting the value of mixing with them in their off-duty hours, showing feature films myself on our projector in one of the larger rooms and, perhaps best of all, going out in the night at all times when bombs fell, to be with them as they too turned out, if they were off duty, to help with the rescue work. All this not only helped me to identify myself with them but, I think, drew me to them, because they felt I was acting just like they themselves had to act, facing the same kind of dangers. I certainly would not have missed this opportunity for the world. I often wonder what I should feel like now if I had to say that, during the second world war, I lived in the country free from danger. I am glad to have had the privilege with my wife, and for part of the time with my young daughter, together with friends living in the vicarage, to be in London when the Blitz was at its height with bombs falling all round.

I suppose during this time, if I am to explain it in a way that everybody can understand, I was teaching and preaching every Sunday, trying to make clear the gospel of Christ in the situations in which we found ourselves, and how His love called us to respond with love to Himself and to the service of His other children. There were not many occasions when I needed to take a firm stand but I did upon one point. Right through the war I never allowed my congregation in public worship to 'pray for "victory"'. Of course I, like them, believed that part of our reason for fighting was that we were fighting for justice against aggression and tyranny; the victory of the Nazi philosophy over our values would have been disastrous. Therefore, physical suffering was less important than indoctrination of mind and domination of our society. But that did not mean that we could therefore pray as if God was undoubtedly on our side. Naturally we hoped and believed that He desired our victory. But it would be, if we could think theologically, a blasphemous view to be quite certain that God was on our side and to pray to Him to help us overcome our enemies. So, we did not pray for victory, although we prayed for the people who were fighting; we prayed for our enemies; we prayed for those who were suffering; and we prayed for those in the overwhelmed countries such as France and Holland. But for 'victory', just like that, never.

In the course of my preaching, which usually had a series of topics for three or four Sundays running, naturally I made an appeal for commitment to Christ. These appeals meant a prolonged silence after the sermon, when people could make their own personal commitment to Him. I remember an extraordinary occasion. It was the first and only time that I ever called for commitment, but I had a strong conviction that this was what I must do. During the sermon I pointed out that I had been at Holy Trinity, Brompton for about six years. I said that during that time I had never asked for any public witness of commitment to Christ but this morning I was going to do so. I pointed out that I always said goodbye at the west end of the church at the door but today I was not going to do this. I was going out at the top end of the church, the east end. I would stand outside at the bottom of the vestry steps. This meant that if anybody wanted to come to me they would have to walk about fifty yards from the west door, out of which they all came, in the full view of everybody. I said: 'I shall stand there so that everybody will see anybody who comes. If you come, it will mean that during the time I have been here, gradually or suddenly, you have reached the point where you know you have committed yourself to Jesus Christ and want to give Him your love and your service. This public commitment will be a great help to you but also a great witness to the others.' It was a marvellous and moving sight when some two hundred people came – an admiral or two, a colonel, other military people, ordinary people, young people, all sorts and types. What a wonderful witness to the power of the gospel! I am so glad that I offered that opportunity; and some of them told me afterwards what a real blessing it had been to them.

There were not many other occasions on which I had consciously to show moral courage in my leadership, but there was one other that still lives in my memory because it taught me so much and undoubtedly moulded me to some extent. It happened early in the war. I was looking for another colleague because my senior colleague had gone into uniform. About that time I heard of a first-rate young deacon who was serving his curacy in the north of England. He had come alive to Christ during my ministry at Oxford. When I heard about him, I learned that he had been told to leave by his vicar, although he was still a deacon. Jim was a pronounced pacifist and being a man of great conviction he did not conceal it. Why should he? So I wrote to him and asked him to come and see me. We met and I invited him to be my colleague, but I went on to explain to him the special difficulties of Holy Trinity, Brompton. I pointed out that we had a number of military people and their families worshipping every Sunday morning. They were intelligent, thoughtful people. I said that I was sure they would understand the position of a pacifist and respect it, but he must not push it down their throats. If he took my advice, he would not go about talking to a lot of people in the parish about his pacifism unless he was asked, and then, of course, he must tell the truth. The pastoral ministry and spiritual work he had to do was surely more important than stating his own position too forcibly.

He listened to me and agreed, although rather doubtfully. So I added: 'Jim, if it is really on your conscience that you must declare yourself publicly as a pacifist then you may do so in one sermon, although you must give me notice in advance. But I hope you will not want to do this.' After about three months he came to me and said: 'I want to exercise that option you gave me of preaching about my pacifism.' I said: 'Well, Jim, so be it. God is blessing your ministry here and, if you wish to do this, then certainly you shall.' So he did. He could not have put it worse for my people. Remember, he was both young and pugnacious. I must just add he matured later on into a brilliant and splendid principal of two theological colleges. He had a tremendous influence in training clergy for the ministry, both at Durham and Oxford. In the course of his sermon he rubbed salt into the wound by saying: 'If I was a layman, I would not fight.' It was a silly thing to say, because he was not a layman and he was not asked to fight.

All hell broke out, as I knew it would. People were furious with him. Members of the congregation wrote to influence the church council, so that I got a letter saying that the PCC requested me to ask Jim to resign. I took no action for the moment. But within two or three weeks I published a course of sermons, the first of which was 'Can a Christian be a pacifist?' The second was 'Christian freedom' and so on. I preached the first sermon myself with great enthusiasm, because I was not a pacifist and I shared why I could not be as a Christian. One of my wardens was so enthusiastic that he offered to print the sermon at his own expense and distribute it. I thanked him but did not take up his offer. On the next Sunday morning I asked Jim to be away. Before the service began I invited the members of the PCC to meet me in the vestry. 'Ladies and Gentlemen,' I said, 'I have asked you to meet me just before the service because I am going to speak against you by name and I thought I had better warn you. I am sure you will appreciate this.' I sent the startled group into the church. I got up in the pulpit. I reminded them of last Sunday's sermon and then I said I wanted to preach this day on 'Christian freedom'. I said a number of things about Christian freedom, in the course of which I pointed out that part of the Christian gospel was to enable people to understand that it was God's purpose that we should have freedom of speech and that we must speak the truth as we see it, fearlessly and plainly. I then told the crowded congregation about the letter I had received from the Parochial Church Council demanding Jim's resignation. I added that I did not agree with Jim's point of view, as they knew very well from my sermon the previous Sunday; nevertheless he had a right to hold it and to speak it, if he felt it right. Then I went on to say: 'I will not ask Jim to resign unless the majority of you wish it. I will give you until next Saturday, and during that time a good number of you who are members of this congregation – regular members – will write to me and tell me whether you want me to ask Jim to resign or not.'

God bless their hearts. I received unexpected support, although I thought they would be on my side. But I did not expect that ninety per cent of those that wrote to me – and hundreds did – would be in favour of my standing firm and not asking Jim to resign. That taught me something. It taught me to trust my people and not to 'nanny' them. Tell them the truth with conviction and I think you will find the majority will come behind you – at least that has been my experience. Naturally, a month or two later I had a quiet word with Jim and said: 'Look, I am not going to ask you to resign, because the congregation want you to stay. But don't you think you are discovering you have lost your spiritual influence by that rather pugnacious sermon, and that probably your pastoral work is not as you would wish it to be?' He admitted this. So I said: 'Now, don't resign. But if a good offer comes to you from somewhere else, please feel free to take it and I shall understand why.' I believed Jim learned something from that and I know that I did. I believe somewhere here lies a great lesson to all of us who are spiritual leaders. You have got somewhere to face the truth in such a way that we get some iron into our souls; the iron of speaking the truth, although we know it is going to be unpopular, and yet to speak it regardless.

So, my ten years at Holy Trinity, Brompton were full of joy; of happy, spiritual results as well as of failures and disappointments. They were also full of all sorts of events, some of which I have mentioned already, others which just happened. The church was on fire from a fire bomb. We had to put it out. Our hall was blown to bits by a direct hit. Bombs were all around us, breaking forty windows in the vicarage and bringing some ceilings down. I would drive around London in my car after bombs had fallen, seeing flames around Westminster Abbey, doing all I could to help in any way but being careful to avoid causing any obstruction to the professional rescue teams and fire brigades. All these and many other memories are mine and I would not exchange the experience of the ten years as vicar of Holy Trinity, Brompton, partly during war time, for the world.

6 – New York, November 1948

My first trip across the Atlantic was in 1936. I was invited to take two missions in Toronto in Canada, one in St Anne's, a suburban church, and the other in St Paul's, Bloor Street, a very big church in the centre. I was very thrilled at the invitation, as it was the first time that I had been asked to go overseas. Of course, Win came with me; also four other friends whom I invited to help with giving witness at some of the meetings and with preaching on Sundays, so that we could cover quite a bit of ground. We were given a very good welcome and the missions in Canada, to my mind, went extraordinarily well, because I was unknown and, except for my British accent, had nothing in particular to commend my speaking. However, we filled St Anne's and there were a number of very definite commitments to Christ as far as one can ascertain these matters and also at St Paul's. This building held about two thousand people but the acoustics were dreadful and the sound amplification in those days was not at all adequate. It was very difficult indeed, especially as I tend to go rather fast and get excited in proclaiming the gospel. While I was in Canada, I was invited to go down to Washington to give a series of lectures at the College of Preachers. It was a great privilege and I tried to give some sensible talks on evangelism as I saw it. What made it also rather exciting was that I went by plane from Toronto to Washington and back, the first time I had ever travelled by air.

Before I sailed for Canada, Archbishop William Temple and a very kind young clergyman whom he knew gave me certain introductions which I could use if occasion offered. One of these was to a young theological professor. According to the Archbishop he was the best young theologian in America – high praise indeed. So, while I was in Washington, I went to Virginia Theological Seminary to see Dr Charles Lowry. We talked theology late into the night. I remember at one point saying to him: 'Charles, tell me this. How is it that I, who have nothing like your intellect, and only a fraction of your knowledge of theology, can keep up a sense of conversations by questions and comment, besides making my own personal contributions? How can I keep up with you? I cannot understand why I can.' Charles replied: 'Oh, that is quite easy to explain. I may know my theology and I may be much more academic than you are. But you know your Bible and you know the inner meaning of what the Bible teaches. This is the knowledge which enables you to keep talking with me on a level, as it were.' I shall always be grateful to Charles for that remark, because it showed me that to know the inner meaning of the Bible is what really matters.

About twelve years later, I was in a suburb of Washington taking a series of talks in Charles Lowry's church, for he had now become a rector. He introduced me in his usual forthright way and perhaps I shall not be immodest if I quote his exact words: 'It gives me great pleasure and a sense of privilege to introduce our speaker for a series of lectures – Canon Bryan Green of Birmingham, England. I am sure he will not mind me saying exactly what I think of him, because we are very great friends. He is not a good theologian nor is he a deeply reflective intellectual person; but he does have a clear mind and communicates his thoughts most articulately. Above all else he, more than any other man I know, is able to preach the gospel of Jesus Christ sensibly and attractively.' I was deeply touched by his words at the time and they have been a support to me ever since. From Virginia Theological Seminary I went back to Toronto.

My return across the Atlantic was not until 1944 and it happened like this. I was in London throughout the Blitz, and from 1939 until 1948 I was chaplain of the Communications Control Centre of the Anti-Aircraft Defence of London which was situated underground in my parish in West London. Because of this, I was invited by the Government to go officially across Canada and talk about radar mechanical gunnery – rather strange, because I knew very little about it technically but enough to explain it reasonably to people more ignorant than myself. Behind that was the purpose to boost the morale of the RAF and other military groups training in Canada during the latter part of the war. Naturally, they worried about the rumours from home. What happens when the Flying Bombs and then, later, the rockets descend on London? I was sent out to go around and talk, giving first hand news. I enjoyed it thoroughly, because being on an official visit I was welcomed and made at home at each place to which I went, and often flown around Canada by the RAF or the RCAF. I enjoyed meeting the military people and found them a simply splendid crowd. Also I got the opportunity (because I made it) of giving some evangelistic talks. I made contact with the Anglican Church and wherever I went they were expecting me to be there, so that I could fit in a visit with them together with my military commitments. It was a thoroughly good programme and I would not have missed it for the world.

I mentioned that I was often flown around by the RAF. On one occasion my pilot was also a peace time aerobatics instructor in the RAF. As we got into the plane he said casually to me: 'Are you air sick? If not, do you mind if I do a little aerobatics during our flight together?' I replied very carefully and honestly: 'No I am not, so please do the aerobatics. I shall enjoy them.' As we approached our destination, he suddenly started his aerobatics, flying upside down, looping the loop and all the other pieces of aerobatic flying which he knew so well and executed so perfectly. We landed and I was helped out of the plane looking perfectly normal and not the least disturbed by what had happened and in good form. I noticed that, although he was pleased with how I looked, my pilot was a little disappointed. Later, in the mess, I discovered that it was normal practise with his flying with some civilians to visit an airforce base that he indulged in aerobatics just before we arrived. The result most often was a dishevelled and distraught passenger, feeling very sick and looking very miserable. My appearance and enjoyment of the aerobatics quite disappointed him!

My visit to Canada gave me a real sense of the possibilities and opportunities in the great new land across the Atlantic. Because of that visit I made slight contact with people in New York, especially some who were on the executive of the American

Council of Churches. Among these was that great international missionary statesman John R Mott. I had the privilege of having a lunch given in my honour at which he was a fellow guest. By then he was well over eighty but full of mental vigour and as dynamic as ever.

In 1947 the American Council extended an invitation to me to spend some four weeks in the United States going around to a number of university campuses. I was to be the guest speaker of what were then called 'Religious Emphasis Weeks'. There was always a compulsory convocation, to which all students were expected to come, as all lectures were cancelled for that particular period. Coming from overseas, I had the privilege of giving the convocation address. This was my first contact with what I may call the woolliness of academic Christian thinking. They were so anxious to please everybody, that the chaplains watered down the topic and the messages as far as they could. In one place they carefully said to me: 'Don't say anything definitely Christian. Please speak to the topic, which is "One God, One World"'.

When I got up to speak I could not resist it. I attacked the topic and said: 'If there is a God at all there can be only one God, the ultimate intelligence behind everything; that is common sense. I have dealt with "one God"; and the other, the world, I need not speak about. Everybody knows there is only one world although there may be other worlds which we do not know anything about. So that disposes of the topic. This enables me to get on with what I really want to say. I will try to explain to you why I am a Christian and why I think Christianity is the truest and best way of knowing about God and coming to a relationship with Him.' You could have heard a pin drop. I realised the fellow members of the team were furious with me and I had deliberately thrown a cat among the pigeons; but, on the other hand, the students were fascinated, because plain English speaking was just what they longed to hear. When I finished I got a standing ovation and the first person to congratulate me on my speech, believe it or not, was the Jewish Rabbi. He said: 'Bryan Green, it was good to hear a Christian not afraid to state his faith clearly and plainly; at the same time making quite clear that you understood that people will disagree with you.

I am thoroughly with you.' So I had one supporter in the team, a Jewish Rabbi against the liberally-minded, woolly protestants. This helped me because from then onwards I realised that, in evangelism especially, with young people and students you must be absolutely clear-cut and definite about where you stand. They respect integrity. They respect conviction, as long as what you are saying sounds both sensible and is openly tolerant; that is to say, you do understand there are other ways of thinking and you are merely stating the truth as you see it – but stating it with conviction. I believe this is a fundamental point for evangelism. Again and again in this autobiography I have emphasised this point about integrity, linked with an understanding tolerance, the gospel being sensible and yet inclusive with others who seek God in a rather different way. He finds them, because God has many ways of finding people.

So I arrived back home. A month later, much to my surprise, I received a letter from the Bishop of New York. During my visit of 1947 I had briefly visited New York and preached in two churches there. This caused the invitation to come to me. It was asking me whether, in November the following year, I would lead a Gospel Preaching Mission in the Cathedral of St John the Divine in New York. I knew the Cathedral was vast and only a few yards short of St Peter's, Rome, holding something like six thousand people. I found that prospect rather daunting. Nevertheless I was pressed to accept, so I did. Later on, I discovered why the invitation came to me. It was very instructive. Two men had been praying for about five years together that God would bring some revival by the gospel to New York and in particular to Manhattan. The two men were Sam Shoemaker, who had been in the Oxford Group but had now broken away from it, a very definite Low-Church evangelical, and the other was his great friend Father Tabor of the Church of St Mary the Virgin, an extreme Anglo–Catholic. As committed Christians, they were very deep personal friends and so they had been praying together every fortnight for the revival of religion. Together they had gone, I learned later, to the bishop of the diocese and asked him to invite me. I planned that I should go to New York for three weeks, which would give me fourteen days or so before the ten-day mission began. Then difficulties arose. It so happened that in June of that year I was invited by the patrons to become Rector of Birmingham. This was a great privilege and honour. I at once accepted. Bishop Chavasse, the chairman of the patrons, was very understanding. He immediately accepted my point that I could not go until after I had fulfilled the engagement in New York in November, so that 1 January was the earliest date I could take up my post in Birmingham. The other patrons were not nearly so understanding and tried to persuade me to change my mind. I absolutely refused and said that, if that was their condition, then they must get somebody else for Birmingham. However, in the end they gave in and presented me. Bishop Barnes, with whom I got on splendidly throughout the few years he remained as our bishop after I got to Birmingham, could not have been more helpful or understanding. He arranged to institute me as Rector of Birmingham, quite unusually, in September. From that moment, I gave up any income from Brompton, but he allowed me to go back to Brompton to take services there, as well as to go to America, taking up my job as Birmingham rector after Christmas. During that time Bill Codrington was my able curate. He had been a chaplain in the Royal Navy and got sunk with the Ark Royal. He did magnificent pastoral work amongst the sailors and was a very brave man. He held the fort in Birmingham for me.

This difficulty over, I enjoyed my last few months in Brompton. I was very sad indeed to leave, though quite sure I was right in doing so.

I found as I expected that the Episcopalians had no idea how to organise and promote an evangelistic mission. It was not their cup of tea. Believe it or not the posters were not issued to the clergy of Manhattan to put up in their churches until ten days before the mission started. In fact, shortly after we got there, we were having dinner with the bishop of the diocese, Bishop Donegal, who said to my wife in my presence: 'I hope some people will come up to hear Bryan on Sunday week.' So did I. I nearly said: 'Well, that is why I have come; if they do not turn up, what is the point of having me anyhow?' But I refrained. It showed the lackadaisical approach.

However, I had to do something about it. Directly I arrived I went for four or five days to Poughkeepsie. The rector there at the time was the man soon to become very famous, the Reverend James Pike. We became great friends. Years and years afterwards on television, he told me that working alongside me was his first insight into what evangelism really meant. It was a privilege to know him. A highly intelligent person and, in spite of all his critics later on, a really orthodox man as far as the gospel of grace was concerned, he was too forthright, too provocative and loved the limelight of television. I quite see why he had enemies as well as friends; nevertheless, a man of his type had to be a kind of gadfly. He kept on prodding other people, if that is the right word for a gadfly, or stinging other people is perhaps more accurate, into action. He challenged the more pedestrian, the more sleepy of the Episcopal clergy and laity by his way of putting things. You can imagine, therefore, that we had a great time in his parish and a real response to the preaching of the gospel. But it was not just in his parish that the interesting things happened. The real event of some importance for the mission later on was that I was asked to go and speak at Vassar College; then it was an all women's college – very intelligent, very snooty and not at all inclined towards religion. The full-time chaplain was vague and woolly. I shall never forget the way he introduced me: 'It is very nice of Bryan Green to come today and tell us where he has got so far, in his search for a meaning to life and for Truth.' I am afraid I was not very polite in my response. I told the story of a small girl who loved hide and seek. She went out to a party. When she came back her mother said: 'Darling, did you enjoy yourself?' 'No, Mummy, I did not enjoy it at all.' 'But why not, darling? Did you not like the games they played?' 'Oh, yes, Mummy, but you see it was all seeking and no finding.' I said I was not one of those just seeking the way of Truth. I believe I had found it in Jesus Christ. It is about Him I was going to talk now; I believe that in Jesus Christ we find God as we can find Him nowhere else. You could have heard a pin drop amongst the students, although I sensed that the chaplain was furious and so were others of the faculty. In fact, so furious were some of the faculty that three of four lecturers the next day spent their time attacking me. One, believe it or not a professor of philosophy, ended up his lecture by this classic remark: 'So you see, any good Hindu can be just as good a Christian as Bryan Green.' For an understanding of philosophy and logic, you cannot beat that for stupidity, can you?

Nevertheless, the opposition was helpful. I had one more lecture there that night, a voluntary one. The place was packed with students. I went to town again with a definite plea for commitment to Jesus Christ and the response to God's love in Him. So I left and went down to New York. Among other things that I did in New York was a whole week of lunch-hour talks – Monday through Friday, at Trinity Church, Wall Street. By then, I think what had happened at Poughkeepsie and Vassar had created some interest because we had a full church the first lunch hour; it continued full and became even fuller with people sitting on the floor on the Friday. I am afraid I was not very tactful. I just spoke out forthrightly about Vassar and the situation, particularly the stupidity of the philosopher and the waffliness of the chaplain. The President of Vassar was furious. Without my realising it, the matter got such publicity that the old graduate students of Vassar, many of them very strong Christian Episcopalians, wrote to the President, upset that the chaplain was so radical and demanding his resignation; in the end they forced this. So, perhaps I did some good by going to Vassar but I was forbidden officially to go on the campus again. Nevertheless, Jim Pike, who rose to all these situations, hired a cinema on the edge of the campus owned by a Jew, who let him have it free for the purpose. There I went up one evening. It was packed with students and I replied to those critics on the campus, defending the uniqueness of Jesus Christ and his finality as God's revelation of Himself to man. Incidentally, this brought Jim Pike into the news and because of that he became Dean of New York Cathedral and finally Bishop of California. It was an interesting string of events, in which I had some small part.

Without my realising it, all this news was building up interest in the mission, now very near and almost upon us, in St John's Cathedral. The Roman Catholic Cardinal, the Archbishop of

New York, had said to the Episcopal Bishop of New York: 'You won't fill your Cathedral, only we Catholics could fill ours, St Patrick's. You certainly won't fill yours.' I rather agreed with the Roman Catholic archbishop, because there was very little interest as far as I could see. Every week day, when I came back from Pough-keepsie during the twelve days or so that were left before we started in the cathedral, I was doing 'one-night stands'. The Suffragan Bishop, a splendid fellow, came with me both to chair the one-night meetings and to give the blessing. With him came a fine young Anglo–Catholic priest with a splendid voice who led our singing. We had a brief service, some singing and then I preached each night in a different church. It was hard going but we were reaching people. God blessed what I said, because they were interested by my British accent, which was rather unusual in those days. Remember it was just after the war and there were not nearly the number of visitors across the Atlantic as there are these days, when the British accent does not mean nearly so much. Perhaps also I was unusual because I tried to make the gospel sound sensible. There was not much to report upon these one-night stands, although they are difficult, because the speaker has got to acclimatise himself to a new group of people each time and they have got to acclimatise themselves to him. You have got to try to sense where the message can get home to them; you know nothing about local situations; you are rather speaking in the dark. That is why preaching the gospel to your own people, your own congregation week after week, is such a privilege and such a great advantage.

But it had to be done, so I tried to do it. One horrible rainy night, I went to a church on the northern tip of the diocese. Quite a number turned up, because they knew the bishop was coming also and they listened reasonably well. At the end of my gospel address we had the usual silence and then I said: 'And now the bishop will give us God's blessing.' Then, suddenly, I had a deep intuition. Fortunately I very rarely get them. I have only had this one once, I am glad to say. I broke in just as the bishop was beginning to speak: 'No, Bishop, please don't give the blessing; for some reason these people cannot have God's blessing tonight.' I turned to the congregation and said: 'Go home please.' I went into the vestry feeling a most utter and absolute fool, dreading to meet the bishop, because he was pretty angry at being treated in the way I had treated him. I apologised and said: 'I am so sorry but this was a deep conviction and I had to say it.' Then I discovered why. The truth came out that for two years the churchwardens had not spoken to the rector; there was a complete division amongst the people with bitter and unhappy feelings all the way round. So my intuition about the situation was right. What followed was extraordinary. When the mission started in the cathedral night after night a coach load of people came from that church. God so blessed that congregation through the mission that the wounds were healed and the place became alive as a true Christian worshipping centre. I am glad I do not have to do that sort of thing very often, because it is not only a question of courage: it is a much deeper matter. Are you right in saying such a thing? Are you right in acting like that? How can I be sure? I think I am right but how can I know?

So the day of the mission dawned. I preached somewhere on the Sunday morning; I think it was at St Bartholomew's, a grand, wonderful congregation. When you got to know them, they were fine and sincere people, most of them. At first sight, the two thousand people looked like a mass of fur coats, very affluent and somewhat snooty. I well remember how I started that sermon. I do not think I was fair to them, but I had a strong conviction that I had to start like that. I can assure you I have never started like that before nor since. These were my very words. I shall never forget them. I said a word or two about being pleased to be present and for their welcome. Then I said: 'I have a feeling that Jesus Christ would be unhappy in this church.' You could have heard a pin drop. There was shock beyond all belief. I then went on to point out that self-centred, affluent complacency with one's self was exactly the kind of situation in which Jesus Christ was not at home in His lifetime on earth – nor would He be at home in that kind of situation now. I followed on with a gospel address.

But I was so wrong in my judgement, because these very people, instead of throwing me out in anger and wrath at being misjudged, welcomed my message and most warmly welcomed me. St Bartholomew's became my favourite church in New York, and I have since preached there many, many times. It may have helped them to hear what I said. It certainly helped me. I was shown a kind of generous acceptance and forgiveness for my brash approach for which I can never be too thankful. I learned; perhaps they did too.

I went back, as far as I can remember, to lunch with the bishop, with whom Win and I were staying and, after lunch, Canon West, the Master of Ceremonies at the Cathedral, telephoned to say that he hoped all would be well that night. He had put curtains up inside the cathedral after the morning service so that there would be space for about fifteen hundred people. 'I am sure that will be more than enough and the people will not look too lost in that vast building'. I agreed with him and I did not think many more would come anyhow, because the Cathedral was situated in a very awkward district of New York and not convenient to reach. It is not very close to residences and people have to travel. However, about six o'clock that evening – we started I think at 7.30pm – Canon West telephoned in a most agitated way from the Cathedral saying: 'Bryan, what shall I do? They are pouring into the cathedral already.' 'Right,' I said, 'Pull down the curtains, what else?' So he did. I went over early and found the place packed, six thousand people seated and standing in all the side aisles; the choir stalls were packed, every inch of space was packed. I did not know what to do; I had never been faced with so large a crowd before; I knew no techniques; I did not know how to handle it. We started with some singing led by another Canon Green, with a lovely tenor voice. He led the singing beautifully, using ordinary Episcopal hymns. While that was happening, instinctively – and this is where being a parish priest with your own people makes all the difference in the world – I had a feeling within me that I had to get to know these people somehow. But how? Six thousand of them! Then I had an idea. I walked right down the length of the cathedral, talking to people as I went on both sides of the centre aisle, chatting, smiling, speaking not loudly but just clearly, making myself known. Then I walked back again. Every night I did this. Although I did not realise this at the time, looking back I see now that I made an important point. From the very beginning I made them feel I wanted to talk to them individually, not as a mass but as individual people, children of God whom He loved, far more greatly than I could ever love them. Then, I began to preach. My sermons did not alter. I just tried to preach simply and clearly. I forget the topics. I chose a different one every night. I tried to make what I said sound sensible. I tried to speak with conviction. At the end we had silence, so that the people could do their own business with God, responding to the gospel as He spoke to them in their hearts and minds. It was extraordinary. Scores of men and women of all ages sought our help afterwards. I trained no counsellors, because I could not plan any follow up. We just had to act as best we could. So I got the clergy together, all that would come, and we went into the large sacristy and elsewhere in the Cathedral, seeing people afterwards and also in the day time, people who wanted to find their way to faith in Christ. Many came. It was a remarkable time with deep and real conversions. After that first Sunday evening the whole of the press was interested. *Time Magazine*, *Life* and the Radio were reporting what was happening. The news was so unusual that in the Episcopal Church at any time there should be this kind of revival mission service. The famous preachers – and there were a number of them in New York – came to hear this strange and unknown speaker as indeed I was. Billy Graham happened to be in New York and he came two or three times. That is where I first got to know him. He himself became famous the following year. My friendship with him means a lot to me. We differ entirely on theology; he is a Southern Baptist and a very conservative type, although he has broadened over the years. I am a liberal evangelical, thoroughly Anglican. But both of us believe in the gospel of God's grace in Jesus Christ as the heart of the Christian faith and that is where we have fellowship together. He preached for me in my church in Birmingham and we have kept in touch ever since. He sometimes has said in my presence, when I have been supporting him at one of his crusades, that the mission in St John's was the first time since World War II there had been mass evangelism in the USA. Indeed he was right and he should know, should he not?

I do not remember very much about individual conversions and happenings. But I do remember what an effect this preaching of the gospel had upon the theological students at General Theological Seminary. They flocked in big numbers to hear the preaching. I was a curiosity and that is why they came and it spoke to many of them. At that time, there was rather a bad moral life in that seminary. It happens in all colleges from time to time. Some of the faculty had been encouraging homosexuality amongst the students. The preaching of the gospel hit home in a place where it hurt and many students and some faculty found the grace of God's forgiveness in Christ and strength for a different pattern of behaviour. As I look back on that mission the thing that most comes clear to me is the power of prayer and God's willingness to use a man just as he is, for you must remember when I arrived I was quite unknown. I had no reputation. I had no publicity value or promotion draw. I was just myself, who was known as a fairly reasonable speaker, a gospel preacher but that was all. It could only have been the work of the Holy Spirit in answer to prayer, for what other explanation can there be for those happenings in New York in St John's Cathedral in November 1948?

I did not realise what this was going to mean but in fact this particular event in New York had two remarkable results – quite unexpected, and certainly not exploited by me, for I did not expect them to happen. The first was that the news went back to England. When I got home and moved to Birmingham after Christmas, because of what had happened in New York, remarkable things began to happen almost at once in Birmingham. The second unexpected result was that invitations poured into me from all parts of the United States from bishops of different dioceses, asking me to take missions for them in their dioceses. From saying 'yes' to them and going to take missions there, as I shall explain in a later chapter, I got invitations to other parts of the English-speaking world and elsewhere.

The reflection that comes from the previous paragraph is simply that I did not seek to be a travelling world evangelist. It happened. Perhaps that is the way it always does happen, if it is God's purpose. We do not seek to be anything, or organise ourselves so that we become something, but somehow or other we find ourselves pushed 'in and in'. Then we begin to see what God wants us to do. I am anxious to put it this way, because I do not want to give any suggestion that I think it is wrong to be an organised travelling evangelist. One of the great qualities of Billy Graham, whose integrity has never faltered from the very beginning, is that he preaches the gospel and has the best possible organisation, both to promote his crusades, so that they are effective with numbers and so on, and counselling to follow up the results of his crusades. This is first-rate organisation, which God honours and blesses. But I believe that the beginning of any man's career as an evangelist, outside his parish or local church, happens to him when he finds himself drawn into it. Whether he is able to follow it up or not depends on his parish and upon him. In my case I was fortunate enough in Birmingham to find a church which understood and was willing to release me each year for three months, in three blocks of a month each, to go to different parts of the world in response to the invitations I received to share the gospel which I was preaching at St Martin's-in-the-Bull Ring.

1956: Bryan Green and the building of the St Martin's Church Hall,
for which he raised over £100,000.

7 – Birmingham Parish Church
St Martin's-in-the-Bull Ring

I arrived back from the mission in New York early in December. The three weeks remaining before I left for Birmingham were very full indeed for me. There were all the normal pre-Christmas activities in Holy Trinity, Brompton as well as saying goodbye to many personal friends and also to the congregation. I do not remember very much about this except that I rushed from one social event to another. I do recall, however, the farewell meeting when speeches were made and presentations given. I vividly remember the speech of the evening was made by my wife. Win does not like speaking very often but when she does she is extremely good. On this occasion she made easily the best speech, in the opinion of many people including myself. It was full of anecdotes about our time at Holy Trinity and very amusing. In her quiet and unassuming way she had been a splendid vicar's wife, doing all she could to help with the work of the church. During the war time period in Brompton she did a good deal of voluntary work, especially working day and night shifts in the police canteen at Scotland Yard. After these farewell meetings came Christmas Day. There was a splendid congregation at the midnight communion and a very full church for the morning service. I could not have had a happier ending to my ministry there. The joy was tinged by much sadness at the thought of leaving such a happy place and so many splendid people and close friends.

Immediately after Boxing Day we began our move to Birmingham. The weather was wretched. There was a good deal of snow about. Because of the shortages in the building trade and the need for licenses to do work an any scale, we found our new rectory in Birmingham with the work of alteration, decoration and so on, unfinished. It was a magnificent house, the gift from the Cadbury family to St Martin's after being originally the home of

Dame Elizabeth Cadbury. There were twelve bedrooms on the top two floors. On the ground floor were three large reception rooms with beautiful Adam windows and a large oak-panelled entrance hall with a magnificent staircase. Then there was the basement with eight rooms. Obviously, this was no house for a rector and his wife. Apart from anything else, staffing was going to be a problem – which we solved by major alterations to the house. Fortunately there were two staircases, the main one and a side stairway at the back of the house to the top floor. We made the top floor into a self-contained flat with three bedrooms, a large comfortable living room, bathroom and kitchen. On the floor below we put in a nice kitchenette and turned two open bedrooms into large and comfortable bed-sitting rooms with a second bathroom. Most of that floor was available for our use. On the ground floor we turned one of the large reception rooms into my study, dividing it with a partition, which became the office for my secretaries. In the basement, two of the rooms were turned into studies for my colleagues, and another large room into a second church office. On the side of the rectory, where the staircase was, we built on an extra room. By doing this, converting an old kitchen and one other room and linking them with the alteration, we made a side flat. This made it possible to have someone living there who was able to help us in the rectory, while her husband was fully employed elsewhere in Birmingham.

This meant that the whole building became useful. We called the official part of it St Martin's House and our private area the rectory. This was a good financial arrangement for the church, because I was able to offer the top flat rent free for one of my colleagues and studies and offices on the same basis. While all this alteration work was being completed after our arrival, I caused some interest by announcing on my first Sunday that I wanted some help in the rectory for my wife – and got it. We did quite a bit of the initial cleaning ourselves. I remember doing some hard work scrubbing floors when the workmen had finished before the carpets were laid. By a stroke of luck, this fact became public and the *Daily Mirror* sent a photographer to photograph the Rector of Birmingham on his knees scrubbing a floor. This gave me a certain amount of interesting publicity.

On my arrival at the beginning of 1949, St Martin's was in a poor state compared to what it had been before the War. This was nothing to do with my splendid predecessor, Canon Guy Rogers. His leadership and ministry before the war had been superb and well known throughout England. During the war, he was courageous both in fire watching and in helping people when homes had been bombed and friends injured or killed. By then he was seventy-two years of age and had not the strength, either physically or mentally, to tackle the job of rebuilding after the war period. The church had been bombed – part of the roof blown off and the west end damaged. This meant the large evening service had to be discontinued, so that all that could be done in the way of worship was on Sunday mornings and in the afternoons during the summer. The congregations had greatly decreased from what they had been. This was the situation that faced me on my arrival. As I mentioned, I came to Birmingham on a wave of publicity, both from the national reports of the extraordinary mission in New York in November, and the personal publicity through asking for assistance and the picture in the Daily Mirror of my scrubbing the floors. The result was unexpected and extraordinary. On the first Sunday morning the church was full, and in the evening packed to the doors, with well over twelve hundred people. It is true that, at my institution a few days before, the Bishop of Birmingham had said in his sermon that I had arrived with a fanfare of trumpets, but I did not expect this result.

I must honestly say that I spent most of that evening service not truly worshipping but busily thinking how I could get a grip on all those people. I had a good idea and rapidly jotted down some notes of two courses of sermons on topical subjects, one for the morning and one for the evening. Then, when I got up into the pulpit, I announced the topics and pointed out that they formed a series and it would be good to come and hear them all. I was wise enough to keep the series to four or five in each case, in order to keep interest moving. By the next Sunday I had prepared and had printed a card entitled the Congregational Roll. On it I asked for signatures of people who would like to promise to try to come to St Martin's at least once a month. I pointed out that I wanted them to give their money to the local church, if they went to one, and to remain loyal members there; and also to help bear witness in the centre of the city, by coming to the parish church at least once a month.

My second Sunday was equally satisfactory, because it had packed congregations like the week before. Everyone received a card and I asked people to sign on the dotted line. This idea had two happy results. It helped to assuage some jealousy amongst my fellow clergy, who perhaps had found the publicity I received to be threatening. It was not very many years, I believe, before all jealousy had died out, because I was not out to poach other people's congregations but merely to maintain a strong witness at the parish church at the centre of the city. The second happy result was that it gave me a large basic membership of people who worshipped regularly from time to time. Very quickly we had seventeen hundred units on the congregational roll; by unit I mean one person who lived on his own or a whole family. As things began to sort themselves out I found that six hundred and fifty to seven hundred were regular week-by-week worshippers at St Martin's and supporters of our financial commitments as a congregation. The other one thousand were people who came off and on, very often once a month as I had asked. This gave me great evangelistic and pastoral opportunity to teach and preach the gospel of Jesus Christ. During the twenty or so years that followed, we had the privilege of having these large congregations Sunday by Sunday, the people coming from all over the area of Greater Birmingham and some even from beyond.

I was now certain of the kind of mixed group which I had longed for when I was in the West End of London. There were people holding high executive office in the many businesses in Birmingham, as well as leading officers in the Council House. We also had some senior members from Birmingham and Aston Universities, together with a number of students. The mass of the congregation comprised middle-class people, together with those working in the factories and shops in the city. As I administered the sacrament, I could see that there were many who worked with their hands day by day, as well as those who were in professions or in an office. Their ages varied, with quite a large number being under thirty. Very soon we also had a flourishing junior church, under the able and dedicated leadership of Bridget Cameron.

At this point I want to make it quite clear that the privileged position of Birmingham Parish Church was not my achievement. It was something I had inherited from the past. Before Birmingham became a diocese in its own right, with its own cathedral, St Martin's dominated the spiritual life of the city. Part of the building went back to 1081 although, owing to two fires, the present building was largely constructed and finished in 1875. Fortunately, there were still some old parts left incorporated very cleverly into the new building. My predecessors had been first-rate pastors and preachers. Therefore, the life and witness of St Martin's had been maintained – even during and despite the war-time difficulties.

So I was given a great opportunity and challenge by a congregation of some fourteen hundred different adults at our three services every Sunday – an opportunity which lasted during the twenty-two years I was in Birmingham. The immediate question was what to do first. I knew instinctively that I could not do it by myself; I must have the laymen and women of the congregation behind me, to help if any spiritual advance was to be real and lasting. In those days the ministry of the laity, as it is now called, was not as common as it is now. So, two or three Sundays after my arrival, I invited any of the congregation who were prepared to meet me in our church hall once a week to pray and plan for the future, to stay behind after the service and about a hundred and fifty did so. I put the plan to them and said I hoped that they would come every Monday evening for one and a half hours to what I was going to call the Monday Fellowship. I imposed one condition: that anybody who came, came every week without fail. If a person could not come on a particular Monday, the obligation was to contact the secretary and offer an apology and a reason. Some sixty men and women turned up on the first Monday. We did not try to increase the numbers by any recruiting, although in fact it did rise and stayed steady at perhaps eighty or ninety.

At this meeting we discussed the policy for the parish on a spiritual level. We would indulge in role play, trying to explain and put across the Christian faith to those who did not believe. We read our Bibles and prayed together. This weekly meeting soon became a closely-knit fellowship of committed Christian people. I want to make it plain that I still discussed matters with the Parochial Church Council, the legal governing body of the church, and with other official people as well. Nevertheless, the Monday Fellowship was the spiritual fulcrum by which I hoped to move the church forward. Within two years, this forward movement began to take place and there was new quickening at all levels in the church's spiritual life. Much to their dismay I informed the members that the Fellowship was disbanded. They were incredulous: 'Why?' they asked. 'Can't we go on? It is a tremendous Fellowship and we do not want to lose it'. My reply was: 'Your work is done. Get absorbed in the ordinary congregation or come to the Bible School which is going to start on every other Monday but there is no longer any need for this spiritual power group to exist as an entity within St Martin's.'

I was sure this was the right decision. At the same time I brought to an end a number of weekly groups, allowing only the fortnightly Bible School and the Wednesday Club to continue. This was a remarkably interesting organisation, which existed before I came to Birmingham. It was led by an extraordinary person, Marian Ashen. The membership remained at around two hundred a week during the time I was at Birmingham. It was entirely social. On alternate weeks we had folk dancing and on the other week we had a lecture, discussion or something of that sort. Undoubtedly it provided an opportunity for people connected with St Martin's who were lonely and needed social friendship. For some time after the Hall was built in 1957, we started and continued the Friday Club to cater for young men and women between the ages of about eighteen and thirty. Somebody said to me: 'Aren't you encouraging intermarriage?' I replied: 'I hope I am', and in fact I was. Quite a number of these young men and women hitched up with each other and formed happy Christian marriages.

After a while, I brought the 8.30 am Holy Communion

service to an end. In the centre of a city it is very difficult to get out and about at that hour. Instead, we held the service at 9.30; it lasted about forty-five to fifty minutes. Most often, it was a communion service. As a general rule, I insisted that the preacher at the 11.00 service would also preach at communion. The only difference for him was that he was given twelve to fifteen minutes to preach then, and up to seventeen minutes at the 11.00 service. The point of having the same preacher was not to save trouble or work; it was to show, symbolically, that both groups of people were one body in Christ though meeting at different times.

After I had been at St Martin's for about eighteen years, I was approached by a Senior Lecturer of Sociology in Aston University. He wanted some of his students to do a survey of the congregation of St Martin's, to find out why they came to St Martin's and what their reactions were. I was delighted that he should do this and gave him every assistance. He came to our services, questioned our people, examined our records and put out questionnaires. At the end of their survey they gave me a copy of their report. I found it fascinating reading. They found that there were three main reasons why people chose to come and worship at St Martin's. They noted that no one of the three reasons was more important than the others, but they all seemed to be basic.

The first reason people gave was the music. They expressed appreciation of the singing by our excellent choir under the leadership of Geoffrey Fletcher, our Director of Music. It certainly was a first-rate choir of men and boys, wonderfully trained and splendidly conducted by Geoffrey. If we sang settings to the canticles, I encouraged the group to sit while the choir sang and to worship by following the words. I never allowed an anthem to be sung unless the words of the anthem were printed in our weekly bulletin. There was an anthem at most services; in announcing it I used to say: 'Please turn to your service papers and follow the words of the anthem while the choir sings. In this way you can worship God.' There was a real point in printing the words and the announcement: it forces people to see that if you hear music as a choir's offering to God it can be a real act of worship. The choir appreciates this very much indeed and bit by bit so does the congregation, as they learn to enjoy music, even if this sort of listening is new to them. When people said they enjoyed the music, they also linked it with the fact that they were allowed to sing as a congregation because, except for the particular things the choir did on their own, all other singing, was by the congregation led by the choir. I was insistent about this. Frequently, we would practise hymns, especially if they were new tunes, three or four minutes before the actual service began. The result of all this was to get a sense of real participation by the congregation in all the singing and in listening to the choir singing for us, as well as by participation in the prayers and other parts of the service.

The second reason people gave for coming to St Martin's was the fellowship. They felt welcome, and were made welcome, and in the end were helped to feel part of the total fellowship of a large congregation. We accomplished this by having one or two people at the door of the church – outside if the weather permitted – to welcome people as they came in. The clergy who were not preaching were at the back of the church too, which made people feel at home. We cleared a space there, so that people could move freely around the back near the book stall. While I did not encourage over much conversation before the service began, afterwards I wanted people to talk to one another and feel perfectly at home. In addition, as soon as we could finally get the facilities, we had tea and coffee after all services in the hall next door. All this helped to make our worshipping community a real fellowship in spite of the size of the numbers. I believe this sense of fellowship was deepened by the fact that, after some years, we had twenty-four house groups meeting in different parts of Birmingham, so that our members could meet in small groups of ten to twenty, thus being able to share their Christian faith more easily with one another and feel bound together closely when they worshipped on a Sunday at St Martin's.

The third reason for coming to St Martin's was given as the preaching. There is no doubt that we took preaching seriously and that applied not simply to myself but also to all my colleagues. I insisted upon very careful preparation and a really keen and committed attitude to the opportunity of offering the gospel by word of mouth during the sermon. As I have already said, we allowed about seventeen minutes at our 11.00 am service for the sermon, but in the evening this limit was increased to twenty-five minutes. Because we expected the people to listen as we spoke, they responded and did exactly that. This is one of the insights about evangelism I have had from my pastoral experience in a parish. If we are going to preach the gospel, it is much more effective if it can be done in the expectant atmosphere of an expectant congregation. Our people settled down expecting to hear the truth when we preached. They were therefore ready to listen and to receive what they could.

Let me explain a little more about our policy for preaching. In the first place, we very soon evolved the idea of producing two series of sermons, usually not more than five in each series, one for the morning and one for the evening. These series were of all kinds. They might be about a Bible character; they might take one book of the Bible and certain chapters of it; they might address temporary problems of moral attitude and so on. There is plenty of room for variety here and the topics were hammered out at our staff meeting on Monday mornings. We worded the topics in ordinary, every-day English with no fancy titles. We printed them on a simple flyer available for our congregation to distribute to their friends. They were encouraged not only to distribute the flyers but to invite their friends to come with them to hear the series. Incidentally, the value of the series is that, as on the radio or television, if the people like the first one they are more likely to come to the rest.

For me, preaching means really 'teaching–preaching'. Whoever gives a sermon must teach the truth as well as proclaim it by forceful communication. This means the teaching can be very varied. It can roam across the whole spectrum of the biblical revelation. It can touch on contemporary problems and moral situations; it can move freely but teaching it must remain. That is the content of the sermon. If that is communicated with conviction in an interesting way, then as we preach we convey the truth in some form or other to our hearers. This is where the attitude of a preacher comes in; does he or does he not expect something to happen? Perhaps more important still, do the committed people in the congregation expect something to happen, as he speaks the truth as powerfully and plainly as he can? That is why I frequently ended my sermons with two or three minutes of dead silence, and my colleagues tended to follow suit, although not usually for as long as I did. I found they were a little frightened of silence! It always seems to me that the truth properly proclaimed demands a response, which is really what one means when one talks about an evangelistic appeal. It is neither a special technique nor a special phraseology; it is really telling the truth of God's Word and then being silent before God, so that people can respond.

Over the years, it was this kind of response that was made during the ordinary services of St Martin's week by week. If you can classify our congregation, a large number were committed Christians, who came to worship and to receive any help they could in deepening their Christian lives. Together with them came a number of church-goers, most of whom were probably baptised and many of whom were Christians in a very genuine way, but not truly awakened to Jesus Christ in whose name they had been baptised. With these two groups came another large group of irregular church-goers – casual you may call them – who came from the university because of the reputation of St Martin's or because their friends brought them. Clearly, there was an opportunity here of helping people on in the Christian life, as well as a very big evangelising opportunity in the atmosphere of worship, so that people who had never been brought to the point before found themselves coming to a place where they made a personal commitment to Jesus Christ as their Saviour and Lord. This is true evangelism and in some ways the best kind of evangelism, because those who are moved can then so easily go on developing within the worshipping community where the light dawned.

Before I leave the subject of preaching, there is a point of policy which I think is valuable. As I have said, we had three opportunities for preaching every Sunday. Only very rarely would I take the three myself. It is perhaps true to say that I was the best known preacher of the team. Nevertheless, I thought it important that my colleagues should develop their preaching gifts – and I am glad to say they did this splendidly. Most of the time I had four colleagues – a senior one and three who came to me straight from theological college. I usually preached at the morning or evening service each week. My senior colleague had more turns than the others but everyone got a chance. In addition, of course, there were various other speaking opportunities in the church programme and I always encouraged my colleagues to accept invitations to preach in Birmingham. They received quite a number and I think preached acceptably where they visited.

On the subject of my colleagues, from the beginning it seems to me that my senior colleague ought to be given special status and importance. An ancient custom in old parish churches was the position of Lecturer. This used to be the case at St Martin's. I revived it and about three years after I arrived I persuaded George Potts to come and take this position. George was a very remarkable clergyman in many ways. His hobby was watercolour painting and he exhibited in the Royal Academy and was made president of the Birmingham Watercolour Association soon after his arrival. He was an excellent preacher, with quite a different style from my own. We did not agree very often on theological matters; his churchmanship was 'higher' than mine. I cannot speak too highly of the splendid band of colleagues I had during my twenty-two years at Birmingham. A great deal of what happened there in spiritual advance and blessing was due to their prayerful and devoted work, based on good professional skills. I certainly could never have gone away happily three times a year on my overseas evangelistic work had I not had the strong team at home, not merely to hold things together – which indeed they did – but to keep moving forward steadily doing the work of Christ. I have often said, rather flippantly: 'My ego would not have allowed me to go away and let down St Martin's'. That may have been true but, more profoundly, I felt real responsibility for doing the job properly to which I had been called and for which I was paid. But I did not have to worry. Nothing awkward happened while I was away, although I am glad to say my people were pleased to see me back. On return I found a united front and steady advance. A rather amusing comment was made to me by a man in the congregation: 'Of course, we miss you when you are away, but I must say your colleagues do splendidly. When you come back, even if you are there to give out the notices, we feel as if we are all together again in peace at home.'

In addition to the Sunday services at St Martin's there were a number of other definitely evangelistic pastoral activities. The St Martin's Monday Lecture happened fortnightly. It was attended by about eighty people, and was taken for three or four years by George Potts who went for a definitely scholarly exposition of the Bible. After a while we decided to change the pattern. This was a common occurrence at St Martin's. We were always willing to change from one thing to another, varying our approach imaginatively. The change here was that we decided to invite a speaker from the Faculty of Theology at Birmingham University, provided at no charge under their extra-mural scheme. The lecturers covered a variety of subjects for eight sessions running. It might be on a Christian doctrine, for example, or on the Atonement, or on Church History and so forth. It seemed to us a pity that, with experts so readily available at hand, we should spend time preparing carefully thought-out lectures for the same purpose. One of us was always present to take the chair at the lectures, which were followed by questions.

Questions also sometimes happened after a Sunday sermon. We handled this in various ways. Sometimes people simply wrote down questions and they were collected at the same time as the offertory. The preacher then received them and gave the answer from the pulpit, having first read out the question. Alternatively, we would collect the questions and answer them in the hall at the beginning of the coffee hour. The most interesting method was when one of my colleagues had a roving microphone and went down the church allowing people to ask their questions through the amplification system. I heard it in the pulpit and answered back. If people were a bit too shy to say it themselves, they said it to my colleague, who repeated it through the microphone. We all felt that this kind of comeback through a sermon was a very valuable learning experience, if it was properly handled and the questions were honestly answered.

Another innovation, which came off, was the Saturday afternoon Shoppers' Service. It was my wife's idea, when she saw the thousands of people milling around outside St Martin's, visiting the stalls and the shops. We started it about a year after I arrived, and it is still continuing today. During that period the numbers attending varied between about one hundred and three hundred but the type of attendance has remained the same. Some are obviously people from other churches who happen to be shopping, but many of the others are people who come in straight off the streets, perhaps tired from their shopping, to sit down and rest and to listen, sometimes out of curiosity. But, in one way or another, we got them in and, over the years, reports filtered back to us of people who had begun to find faith in Christ through those Shoppers' Services and had then linked with their local churches as regular members. Usually there were three of us on a given Saturday afternoon. One of us spoke to the crowds through the loud speakers from the church tower. The other two moved among the crowds, talking to the barrow boys and to the shoppers in a friendly fashion, inviting people to go in. We always made it clear that we started at 4.00pm promptly and ended equally promptly at 4.15pm.

The service itself was exceedingly simple, always with the same format. A familiar hymn followed by five minutes by the clock for a simple, direct address. I remember on one occasion taking over three months, week by week, explaining the Lord's Prayer clause by clause. The talk was followed by a few simple extempore prayers for home, family and so on; then we had a second hymn and the blessing. After I left there was an added improvement, by offering people a cup of tea in the hall if they cared to wait a little longer when the service finished.

I always found taking this service a great privilege and opportunity. Sometimes, amusing things happened. I remember on one occasion a friendly man, the worse for drink, walked up the church while I was speaking and tried to climb in the pulpit and join me. I stopped, and with a friendly smile said: 'Brother, there is not room for two of us here in the pulpit and as I am speaking I must stay. Why don't you sit in the front pew down there and I will come and talk to you in a moment?' He did just that and so did I. On another occasion I noticed a group of six 'Hell's Angels' – the jargon in those days for the leather-jacketed motor-cyclists. They came in out of curiosity, I imagine, with their girlfriends. It was about five minutes before we began and they were laughing and talking rather loudly and self-consciously as one might expect. So I went up to them with a smile and said: 'Glad to see you in here. What brought you in?' 'It's quieter in here than outside and different' was the reply. I said: 'Well, I am glad it is different in here. It ought to be. It is God's House, you know.' Then I added: 'We are going to sing a couple of hymns. Do you know any?' Great consternation. One girl said: 'Isn't there an 'ymn with scattering in it?' 'Oh yes,' I said, 'a good harvest hymn, "We Plough the Fields and Scatter".' 'Yes that's it,' said the girl. 'Well, we'll have it.' I said, although it was not anywhere near harvest. 'But we have two. Does anyone else have a suggestion?' Again, an embarrassed pause then one of them piped up: 'Ain't there one about God of Mercy?' 'Good for you,' I replied, 'I expect you mean "God of Mercy, God of Grace".' 'Yes, that's it', said the same voice. 'Well now,' I said, moving away, 'we are going to start; but mind you people stay here to join in the singing, now you have chosen the hymns.' So they settled down and I started the service. I mentioned the two hymns that had been chosen by some friends of mine at the back, a remark which received applause from the group. Both hymns were sung well and the group listened superbly well. As they left with friendly smiles they said to me: 'See ya!' Whether they came again or not I cannot say but I expect so. We often had a number of young people at that particular service.

Another experiment which I started and which continued for about eight years was the epilogue. It was during the summer only, to start with, and began at nine in the evening for half an hour. At my request John Jobson, who at that time was the manager of the main branch of Boots in Birmingham, ran this. He did his job magnificently and we had up to two hundred younger people each week. We were aiming at people who had been out cycling or walking on a Sunday and could drop in on their way home. Judging by the number of bicycles that were piled up at the back of the church, we got the people we were wanting. We decided later to extend the summer epilogues to autumn and winter. Unfortunately, John Jobson left Birmingham but his place was magnificently taken over by Dennis and Betty Porter. They were a young, committed Christian couple who had been influenced by Donald Soper – later Lord Soper – in the Order of Christian Witness before they came to Birmingham. Under their leadership the epilogues went steadily on and were a very valuable addition to the work of St Martin's. When Dennis left to take up another appointment, it seemed to most of us that it was a time to let the epilogues end.

I believe that one of the marks of a living church is that it accepts and welcomes change; part of this change is to allow something to die when it has done its work. The church, like the world, is littered with organisations which have been immensely valuable during their time, but have continued long after that. For instance, when I came to St Martin's I found a tiny branch of the Girls' Friendly Society, a splendid organisation once, then a dying body. The members, if you can believe it, were all over sixty and there were only six of them.

I mentioned our junior church earlier under Bridget Cameron. It was a great success and between sixty and a hundred boys and girls under twelve met every Sunday morning, while the adults were at the main worship. Bridget was very good with them and it was run like an ordinary church service for children with their own officers. They were taught, however, in classes according to age, which was sensible. Bridget was very insistent – a policy I thoroughly agreed with – that nobody should be forced up to the main adults' service, unless they wanted to come. This did not delay them over long, when they ought to have been up with us. It worked naturally and simply on a voluntary basis of change. Looking back, I am sure that I did right in allowing the junior church to continue as it was under her guidance and she continued after I left. There were problems, which I had seen, but on balance, ignored; the children did not learn to take part at all in adult worship. The simpler and older form of children coming in for some of the adult worship and then going out for Christian instruction is a better procedure.

One striking experiment must be mentioned. Some of my young people who were very committed Christians had made friends with some of their peers, who worshipped at the Pentecostal Assembly not far away. We had excellent relationships with our fellow Christians of all denominations during my time in Birmingham. My own people approached me and said: 'Do you think the PCC would lend us the Hall for a meeting on Sunday nights about 9.00pm for an hour?' I said: 'What do you want it for?' They replied: 'Well, with our Pentecostal friends we plan to go round the pubs and cafés in the neighbourhood and get young people under twenty and over fourteen to come and have coffee in the hall and then we can talk to them about Jesus Christ.' I was intrigued by the idea. With some trepidation I mention it to the PCC, because our Hall was panelled and was a very prized, beautiful and well-used possession. I rejoiced that the PCC agreed unanimously that they should have it free for the year. The only condition was that at least one of the clergy should be there. I advised that there should be two clergy there with their cassocks on; outsiders like to see clergy in cassocks, I believe. They recognise it is a uniform of authority and, provided that the wearer is friendly and outgoing, they do not resent it. The very first meeting was a success. There must have been one hundred and fifty there, of whom only about thirty were the Christian organisers. It was very noisy but perfectly orderly. As I anticipated, they respected the premises and the surroundings. I think the only damage done in the year was a broken chair and a broken table. After the coffee and socialising the meeting started. I was amazed. The young people, mostly the pentecostalists, because mine were a bit too scared to do it, spoke to their peers. The speaking was very peculiar to my mind. It was very biblical. I could not believe the peers understood it; but it was most sincere and from the hearts of the speakers. Watching closely, as I did, I could see that, contrary to intellectual expectations, what was being said was going home; the others were listening. Afterwards, people stayed to discuss and ask questions. It is difficult to assess the spiritual results of such an effort but I do believe that a number did find faith in Christ; certainly many listened, probably for the first time in their lives, to honest speaking of the Christian gospel.

Early on, the pentecostalists and my young people came to me and asked me to speak. I was perfectly honest. I replied that I was too frightened to face it. They said: 'You, frightened!' I said: 'Yes, I am not one of them. You can speak in the way you do and use the phrases you use and get away with it, because you belong to them, in their age group and in background in many cases. But I could not get away with it, so I am not going to do it and I am perfectly happy that you should go on doing it. It is your effort and God is blessing it.' They did not ask me again nor did they ask any of my colleagues! After a year we allowed this experiment to end.

As St Martin's was the parish church of Birmingham, a great number of special services took place. Fortunately they were usually on Sunday afternoons. The visitors normally chose their own outside speaker, and used our choir, although I was especially invited. We had a rule, however: one of the local clergy should be present, to welcome the speaker and to take charge of the orderliness of the service. I believe this is not only a courtesy but also necessary to uphold the dignity and propriety in what was done in a central church like ours.

I found, coming to Birmingham, a fairly well attended lunch-hour service on Thursdays, lasting for three quarters of an hour. I continued it and it still continues today. But the numbers have gone down a great deal and for two very good reasons. First, the lunch period in Birmingham has been greatly reduced in time span. The more important reason however was interesting and was revealed to me by one of our visiting preachers. He said that he found throughout the country the number at such services was going down. He held that it was because people like himself were often heard on radio and, later, seen on television. The desire to go to see and hear some well-known speaker from London or elsewhere was not the same draw as it used to be. I allowed the service to go on, because it was valuable to those who came and indeed I can remember one man, then managing director of a big factory on the edge of Birmingham, who came in one lunch hour to the service. He used then to come regularly and, finally, at the age of about fifty-five, committed himself to Christ and from then on, he and his family became regular members of St Martin's.

I have mentioned the Parochial Church Council several times. The equivalent in the Episcopal Church in the USA is the Vestry. It is the legal management council of the church, with twenty or so members. Almost immediately on arrival, I put through a resolution at the AGM that a year later (there had to be this awkward gap) we would increase the number to a hundred. I can see now a surprised look on their faces and the gasp of amazement. However, I got my way and pointed out that with the large number of adults worshipping with us on Sundays, a small PCC was hardly representative. The larger numbers at once did what I hoped for. It enabled a great number of people who wanted to be activists in the management of St Martin's to come on the PCC. We did have elections each year but as a rule we found about the right number of people came forward for election as there were vacancies. From my point of view as rector, it changed the whole situation. Legally, I had to take the chair, so I did this at the beginning of each meeting of the PCC, but immediately asked leave to vacate the chair. The vice chairman, always a layperson, took my place. He opened the meeting with prayer and then conducted the business and closed with prayer. This enabled me to speak, if I wished to, during the meeting but did not force me to be always on my feet and, as it were, taking charge. Obviously, the only way to handle business with a large meeting like that was to have a number of committees. These committees met from time to time, although not too frequently, and laid their reports on the table at the PCC four or five times a year. The reports were spoken to briefly by the chairman of the committee and usually passed without delay and without much debate. This procedure got the day-to-day business out of the way, unless there was a specific reason or careful discussion with any particular point. The PCC would then turn to general policy in relation to St Martin's. The discussion and advice that I heard there was exceedingly valuable. I was fortunate to have in my congregation some leading professional men as well as some in business, living and working in the City of Birmingham. The chairman of the Finance Committee was the City Treasurer and working with him was a leading accountant and one of the leading stockbrokers. The finances were managed most smoothly under their guidance.

During my time as rector, we had what my American friends called an 'every member canvass'; we called it the 'stewardship campaign.' There were six dinners in our hall from Monday to Saturday. Each time we were able to seat one hundred and fifty people. After dinner I acted as chairman and introduced two or three speakers, who spoke of the value of carefully praying and thinking out one's duty to give to God's work. They discussed what proportion of that money should be set aside for giving to St Martin's Church under a regular giving plan. After these witnesses, our organisers described how to go to work in thinking about one's pledging and explained that those present could take away a brochure and that during the next fourteen days a visitor would call to answer any questions and so receive their pledge card in a sealed envelope. No one except the registrar, who kept a list of addresses and put a number against each pledger, could possibly trace their envelope back. Everybody received an envelope with a number on it, so as to preserve anonymity when the envelope was opened. The campaign was very successful and we doubled our finance for the next year, which enabled us to meet all our expenses and give a good deal of money to the diocese outside.

In connection with this campaign, something quite important in the spiritual life of the Church happened. At the PCC, I urged the church to have a paid organiser from an outside organisation. I lost the vote. I accepted the decision, although my wife was very angry because, as she said afterwards, the burden would fall on me. Indeed I thought it would. It so happened, however, that just about that time a middle-aged man, very happily married with two children, came to me in a moral difficulty. He told me that the company, of which he was a director and secretary, intended to do something illegal according to a recent Act of Parliament. As a Christian, he asked what he ought to do. 'George', I replied, 'I cannot really advise you, because I have never been in a position when I had to face the prospect of losing my job because I had to stand out on a matter that I thought was illegal and wrong. But I will tell you what I can do. I will pray for you and I will get the congregation to pray for you too, without telling them the circumstances, in case you can be identified. However, if you do come to the decision that you must resign, I promise that I will get the whole congregation behind you – still not knowing who you are – so that we can guarantee an income while you are looking for another job.' A week or so later, George came to me and told me he had felt it right to resign and was now looking for another job. I replied immediately that I would put in motion what I promised. The following Sunday I told the congregation about it, morning and evensong, and asked them to pray that he might find a new job and be reassured that we would stand by him until he found something. Then, a thought occurred to me. I went to George and asked him whether he would take on the organising of our stewardship campaign for twelve months: we should of course pay him. He was delighted and what a splendid leader and director he was. Strangely enough, after about three months he was offered another position and came to me about his dilemma. Fortunately, his new employer was most gracious and allowed George to be seconded to us for a certain period each week, for which, of course, we paid. This testing period was not only a spiritual blessing to George and to myself but also helped the whole congregation to feel they were standing in when one of their number made a costly moral decision.

As I close this chapter there are two or three separate matters, still relating to evangelism, which I wish to introduce. Besides the members of our congregation who wanted their children baptised, a number of parents from a very under-privileged area, which legally was attached to our parish, came to us requesting baptism for their babies. They were completely unchurched and, as far as we could see, had very little intention of changing their habits. Our policy was really straightforward. We believed that infant baptism was justified because of God's unconditional love and that therefore He loves the baby and accepts the baby in and through Christ, even though the parents have no faith or do not practice Christianity themselves. All we asked for was that the parents should be willing to come two or three times to discuss the matter with us. No one ever refused to come and all seemed eager to hear what we had to say, although how much they followed our suggestions I cannot say. I did not feel at the time it was very satisfactory but I was convinced that because of God's grace and unconditional gift to us of His love, theologically I could not turn them away because of the lack of faith of their parents. If we had turned the parents away or refused to baptise, we would have done harm to the gospel of Christ and not helped our evangelism.

St Martin's, being a central church in the centre of the City with people coming to worship from all round in the area, brought some interesting characters. A very simple and a very genuine Christian young woman, with little basic education, worshipped with us on Sundays. When we started the Shoppers' Service, she volunteered to come every Saturday afternoon to give out hymn books. All the time I was in Birmingham and for some years afterwards, she did this faithfully week by week. Whenever I saw her there, I just rejoiced that in a simple, straight-forward way Ivy was able not only to love the Lord inwardly but to serve Him outwardly and consciously with a simple act of welcoming people as they came to that service. A very different kind of person was Graham. He had come, I think, into some faith in Christ when he joined us; then we went away for some weekend with some of the group of Christians and came back 'on fire'. His enthusiasm was immense. What he had discovered during that weekend was to him entirely new and he was quite truly, I think, to use a Bible phrase, 'filled with the Spirit'. But as he talked to me enthusiastically about his experience one Sunday evening, as the people were coming into the Church, he said: 'Look at them all in there. Hardly any of them are born again and are real Christians.' I said: 'Graham, listen to me.' I pointed out the backs of certain people I could recognise and told him their personal Christian story, which I happened to know. I went on to say: 'I do like your enthusiasm. It is splendid and don't cool off but later I believe you will recognise that it may make you judge people over-harshly'. He accepted my slight rebuke; some years after, he told me how right I had been to warn him against making too hasty a judgement – we should accept enthusiasm from certain types of new converts but at the same time, kindly but firmly, point out that they must not make Christian judgements about their fellow Christians. This is an important principle, especially for effective congregational evangelism.

During my earlier years in Birmingham, we went away once a year for four or five years to the Swanwick Conference Centre. This could accommodate about two hundred and fifty people and we filled it on each occasion. We usually got an outside speaker and met in small groups as well. I am sure the experience of living and learning together about Christ and the Christian life brought our people together in a very deep and real way, so that their witness to the outside world was greatly strengthened by this corporate activity of learning. We did not continue it for various practical reasons but I am sure it was one of the things we were right to do initially and then stop. It helped to keep the evangelistic spirit and the desire to share the gospel in the whole congregation.

As I end this chapter I want to state clearly my basic discovery that a parish church with a worshipping community is the very fulcrum of true evangelism as well as of true Christian service in a community. During the twenty-two years I was in Birmingham we had our ups and downs, as all groups of people do, but on the whole I think it would be fair to say that our corporate intention held steady, going out to share the gospel with our friends, as well as preaching it clearly and definitely Sunday by Sunday to any who were with us to worship. For this to happen, it became clear that the quality of the worship must be imaginative, lively and real. With this must go a deep sense of expectancy on the part of all who were worshipping, expectancy that as we worship, as much as when we are preaching or teaching, the truth of God's unconditional love will break through again and again in our midst. From time to time a conviction would come to me that this was a moment to call upon people for some kind of outward witness. Confirmation is a great opportunity but there is need for more than this in the lives of all Christians and especially in many who are on the point of becoming committed Christians.

When this conviction was clear in my mind, I would say to the congregation on any given Sunday: 'It is about five years ago since we had our last act of public witness and during that time a number of you have come, I know, either to faith in Jesus Christ as Saviour and Lord for the first time or to some deeper commitment to Him, which you know about and He knows. Sometimes, in fact, I know because you have confided this to me. I am going to give us all a chance to make such a public witness now during this last hymn. I have chosen a very familiar hymn so that you can sing almost without looking at your books. This is important. For those who are going to get out of their pews and come to the altar rails want you to see them, because they are making a witness. If you recognise any of your friends, of course please be sure to say afterwards how glad you are that they made the witness. For those of you who come up to the altar rails, as soon as the hymn is finished, I will just thank God for the way He has blessed you all and you will know exactly what I am referring to and so will He. Then I shall do the final blessing.'

I would then announce the hymn and say: 'As soon as we start singing, please get up and come.' It is a most moving sight for a pastor to see perhaps two hundred of his people of all ages and types, almost immediately get up out of their seats and come forward. There is no pressure here and no manipulation. Most of them have joy on their faces. It is a privilege for them and a joy, as for us who can estimate the thanksgiving in the congregation as they see what God has done in our midst in the lives of our friends. I am convinced that this is very important in all parish life and should be happening in all local churches where there is a desire to share the gospel effectively with those both within and without the church.

Since my retirement, I have been travelling around a great deal, visiting very many local churches and communities. It is a great regret to me that I have discovered so many new ideas which would have been a great help to me if I could have put them into practice in my own church at St Martin's. I think effective evangelism will be greatly helped if ideas which have been put into practice successfully and have assumed real value in bringing people to faith in Christ are somehow or other circulated among all who are working in local churches. It is not so much books of theory that are needed but newsletters of practical, researched action of what works that will help the ordinary clergyman and laypeople in the parishes. So much of my work has never been original. It has been a careful, if not exact, following of someone who has done something successfully, which I have heard about or seen. If we cannot learn from one another, how can we learn from God as we pray? These two ideas of learning from God and from each other are part of the progress in effective Christian evangelism.

When I arrived in Birmingham I was invited by the Lord Mayor, Sir Charles Burman, to the Town Hall so that he might in private welcome me as the new Rector. He was a charming man and I remember during the course of the conversation he said to me: 'Rector, I hope you won't mind me giving you one piece of advice to follow if you want to make a real mark here in the city. You come from London, where you have had a fine ministry. My advice to you is, don't mention your London experiences at all for two or three years. Show yourself to be completely identified with 'Brum'. As soon as they have accepted you as a true 'Brummie' you will then have a real influence with the people living in the city, with a tremendous pride you will have in this place.'

I took his advice and it paid handsome dividends. After a very few years I was one of 'them'. Wherever I went, no matter whether people went to church or not or whether they went to some other church, I was the Rector. That is how they addressed me, that is how they thought of me. It was a humbling position to be in, because I realised the responsibility it carried and hoped I used it well.

We had a great number of special services each year in the parish church. We had a Lord Mayor's civic service and the police service each year. In addition there were nurses' services and British

Legion parades and so on. We shared with the cathedral for the judges' services, which happened three times each year. Although Birmingham has a cathedral, it is true to say that during my twenty-two years there 'Brummies' looked to St Martin's as a spiritual centre of the city rather than to the cathedral, which was linked with the diocese.

I want to make it very clear that this privileged position of Birmingham Parish Church was not my achievement. It was something I had inherited from the past. Indeed, before there was a Cathedral, St Martin's had dominated the spiritual life of the city. First-rate pastors and preachers had been my predecessors and therefore, even through the war, the life and witness of St Martin's had been maintained.

COME HEAR

BRYAN GREEN

One of England's Greatest Preachers

RICHMOND ARENA
8 P.M. NOVEMBER 10-15

 Sponsored by THE BISHOP'S MISSION • Diocese of Virginia

Bryan Green's ministry in America
by Peter Grothe

Peter Grothe is Professor of International Policy Studies at the Monterey Institute of International Studies. He first met Bryan Green when at Stanford University in 1954. They became firm friends and travelled widely on Canon Green's many USA visits.

Bryan Green's ministry in America

The late Bishop Stephen Neill, church historian, once described Canon Bryan Green as 'the greatest evangelist of the Anglican Church of the 20th Century'. Over a forty-six-year period, Canon Green made approximately a hundred and twenty trips to the United States, usually to preach in segments of two to four weeks. He spoke to hundreds of thousands of persons in parishes, diocesan missions, and on university campuses and, of course, to countless others on television. It is doubtful that anyone who observed Bryan Green most closely during that period would want to contradict Bishop Neill. Indeed, it is not possible to think of any clergyman coming from foreign shores who had such a deep impact on American spiritual life as Bryan Green.

There was a remarkable consensus of those who knew him best. We saw him as 'authentic', as one who was not 'preachy', as someone who was always himself, and as one who, despite his deep Christian faith, admitted to honest doubts and questions. We agreed that he had a brilliant mind, an extraordinary wit, a prodigious energy, superb organisational skills, and that he sometimes relished a good controversy. He had a charismatic personality of Churchillian proportions. Those of us who knew him best don't doubt that he could have been a captain of industry if he had decided to go into business or, very conceivably, prime minister if he had decided to go into politics. He, of course, chose neither business nor politics, and as his close friend, Washington attorney James Bell, said: 'It were as if God had zapped Bryan to be an evangelist to thinking people'.

It was because of the qualities described above, among others, that Bryan Green was so popular on university campuses. He spoke at over four hundred high-schools and to more than one hundred and fifty universities including Harvard, Princeton, Yale, University of California and Stanford. As one Stanford student said:

'Unlike most evangelists, Canon Green doesn't require that you leave your brain at the door'.

I had heard Canon Green preach and lecture more than eighty times at universities and churches in California and other states. The event that stands out most in my memory was the week-long preaching mission that he gave on 'Basic Christianity' at Stanford when I was a student there in 1954. During that week, we saw the quintessential Bryan Green!

The Stanford Chaplain at the time, a lanky, kindly Scot named Rabb Minto, was highly enthusiastic about inviting Green to Stanford but was very worried that not many students would turn out to hear him. This, after all, was during the 'apathetic 50s'. Stanford President Dr Wallace Sterling cancelled all classes and called a rare university convocation so that students would be free to hear Bryan Green during his introductory lecture in Memorial Auditorium – which holds one thousand, seven hundred persons. As they walked across the campus to the auditorium, Chaplain Minto warned Canon Green that there might be a disappointing turnout, because Stanford students generally tended to be apathetic about religion. Indeed, as they got close to the auditorium, Minto's fears seemed to be confirmed. There were seventy or so students milling outside the large auditorium, and Chaplain Minto thought that the doors were still locked. What, in fact, he discovered was that the auditorium was already packed with students; eventually, there were another three hundred standing outside to whom the lecture had to be broadcast.

There was an air of high curiosity and expectation as Canon Green strode on to the stage to begin his lecture. The beginning of his talk was not exactly what students expected:

'The first thing that I should want to say to you is that I am not interested in your nasty little sins. In fact, most of you don't have enough adventure in you to be really big sinners (loud laughter). But what I *am* interested in is THE sin – which is separation from God'.

During the first fifteen seconds, Canon Green had caught the students' attention and curiosity, and during the next four evenings, he spoke to standing-room-only crowds of over two thousand in the Stanford Memorial Church. He displayed the endurance of a marathon runner. In addition to one or two major lectures each day, he would have lunch and dinner bull sessions at student dormitories and then another question-and-answer period at other living residences after the evening lecture. Sometimes these would last into the wee hours of the morning. During the rest of whatever free time he had during the day, he would meet with students individually to answer their spiritual questions. It was estimated that he talked to audiences totalling fifteen thousand. According to veteran Stanford Professor James T Watkins, never before or since have so many students discussed and argued religion on campus. And there was a lasting impact on many.

Bryan Green's major challenge at Stanford, as it was at other universities, was to deal with the intellectual doubts and questions of skeptical students. Occasionally, in response to someone who said that Christianity was all mythology, he would relate a story from the time when he was chaplain at Oxford. He said:

'When I was Oxford Chaplain, sometimes students would come to me and say: "Bryan Green, I don't believe all this Christianity nonsense that you are talking about." And I would say: "Well, that's fair enough, but tell me, what books have you read that are on the same intellectual level with your university studies that try to make the case for Christianity?" Nine times out of ten, students would say that they hadn't read a single book on the subject. And I would respond: "Don't talk absolute rubbish with me! Go out and read a proper book and then we'll have a discussion."'

Canon Green was never known for his tolerance of intellectual sloppiness. He frequently pressed home the point that it was quite all right to question Christianity, as long as people had first studied what it was that they were questioning. He said to a living room of fraternity students: 'If you were to ask me: "Bryan Green, do you like opera?" and I responded: "No, I don't like opera," you would be quite justified in asking me: "Well, have you ever heard an opera?" And I would answer: "No, I have never

heard an opera, but I am absolutely sure that I don't like opera."
Then, it would be quite reasonable for you to say: "Well, how do
you know if you don't like opera if you never heard one?" And, of
course, you would be right! And so it is with religion. These very
bright students mock Christianity, but they have never made the
intellectual effort to find out what it is that they are mocking.'

During his week of question-and-answer sessions with
students, he maintained his directness, his cheerful, upbeat
demeanor, and his dry English wit – all trademarks of Bryan Green
– which helped him to make his points. Further, it helped that he
had an Oxford accent. For some reason, Americans think that
words said with an Oxford accent are more authoritative than if
they are said with an American accent!

In his series of four lectures on 'Basic Christianity', Bryan
Green began with the assumption that listeners believed nothing
and went to the point where they would choose or not choose to
take the leap of faith. His final lecture – to an audience of over two
thousand – had an enormous impact and many erstwhile skeptics
and borderline Christians were led to a definite Christian
commitment that final evening. Canon Green devoted most of his
final lecture to the barriers to faith and used the story of Jonah and
the Whale as his text. (He did not take it literally.) He said:

'You may recall that in the story of Jonah and the Whale
there was a tremendous storm, and the sailors tried to row harder
while Jonah was on board. The storm did not relent. It was not
until the sailors threw Jonah overboard that the storm subsided
and the sea was quiet. Many of you have your own Jonahs on
board tonight. You try to row harder but the storm will not
subside as long as your Jonah is on board. You say: "I'll teach a
Sunday School class". You try to row harder with your Jonah on
board. You say: "Oh, I will give to the Red Cross". You try to row
harder. Or you may say: "I'll read the Bible more". You try to row
harder. But the sea remains stormy as long as your Jonah is on
board.'

Canon Green went on to say that sometimes aspects of
greed or pride are the barriers to faith: 'Too often, you Americans
think that you can "achieve" God. Men and women, don't you

understand – you can not, by your own works "achieve" God. We can never be deserving of God's love, no matter how hard we try. That is the concept of God's grace. He loves us, no matter how undeserving we are of His love. You will simply have to lay yourself open to His love. And so we have to throw our Jonahs overboard. Maybe it is some simple little Jonah that is a barrier to faith – jealousy of some other person, or greed for some material object, or too much intellectual pride.'

And then Canon Green finished his talk with some words that had a greater impact on many persons there – including this writer – than anything I heard him say during the mission:

'But it is not enough to simply throw your Jonahs overboard. You must also let Jesus on board.'

Winthrop Griffith, who was editor of the *Stanford Daily* and who is now an independent writer in Vermont, wrote about Bryan Green's visit to Stanford: 'That generation of Americans was labeled by news magazines as "the silent generation". It was, because of the passive temper of the time, utterly illogical to think that a single man, armed with nothing more than a serious message and challenge, could fill the largest auditorium on campus and the huge church there.

'He summoned and sustained an intense, keen, and profound personal attentiveness by those thousands of students. He reached out to them not as a crowd. He reached out to them as individuals. And I still don't understand how he did it, but I am convinced that he touched each of them individually. I heard countless individuals say what I felt after listening to him. "How did this Bryan Green know *me*? How did he know about my experience, my life? My God, the man sees right into my mind and heart – dark places and fuzzy struggles and bright hopes and all!"'

Bryan Green's ability to speak to doubting intellectuals with directness and integrity, observed by many at Stanford, was duplicated all around the United States from the beginning of his ministry there in 1948 until his last trip there in 1992. Washington lawyer James Bell wrote:

'Both my wife, Jill, and I were converted at a mission which Bryan held at the Washington Cathedral in 1949. I had no intention of going to the Mission. I was invited by a friend the first night and was thoroughly intrigued by both the common sense and spiritual depth of the man. He used down-to-earth language and avoided mystical heights which I could not follow. About half way through the mission I went up to him and said: "I have been very impressed by what you have said. I am now convinced that Jesus was a unique person. Does that make me a Christian?" To my astonishment, he answered: "I'm not going to tell you. You are obviously an intellectual who will just argue with me. Why don't you go home tonight, kneel down by your bed, and ask God, to the extent that you understand Him, to enter your life and show you the Truth?" I did, and He did, and the next night I stood up at the second stanza of *Just as I am Without one Plea* to demonstrate my acceptance of Jesus as my Savior. Bryan obviously did not do this sort of thing very often, but it was extraordinary the way that he could go to the heart of the matter – my pride. Obviously, a graduate of the Harvard Law School, *etc* could figure everything out for himself! Not so, I found.'

Canon Green was fond of saying: 'I much prefer talking to atheists and agnostics than to Christians, because it is no fun if everyone sits around nodding heads and agreeing with each other.' He once spoke to the League of Atheists at Columbia University. The president of the organisation, whom he described as a brilliant and charming woman, was interested in what Green had to say about Christianity, and so she asked if she could have lunch with him the next day and learn more. The result, according to Bryan Green was that 'she became a Christian. It was most disconcerting to the League of Atheists. They had to get a new president!'

Canon Green frequently spoke about fundamentalism during his American tours. He said that he admired fundamentalists for their genuine enthusiasm and dedication, but he despaired at their taking the Bible absolutely literally. He was especially critical of Jerry Falwell's Moral Majority.

In 1981, I invited Canon Green to debate a leader of the Moral Majority at the Monterey Institute of International Studies, a graduate school in Monterey, California where I am on the faculty. The auditorium was packed with students and faculty to hear

Green debate the Rev Richard Zone, who was not only a leader in the Moral Majority but also a clerical campaign advisor to President Ronald Reagan. Green immediately won over the students by announcing at the beginning – with a characteristic twinkle in his eye: 'I suppose that I am a member of the immoral minority'. Rev Zone began by saying that the goal of the Moral Majority was 'to guide this country from the beginning of a Dark Age morally to biblical principles'.

Canon Green said that he admired many members of the Moral Majority for their zeal and enthusiasm. He then proceeded to attack the Moral Majority as 'arrogant, false, contradictory, authoritarian and morally near-sighted. There is no such thing as a plain Christian blueprint for moral judgments. Pacifism and capital punishment, for example, are issues on which good Christians can disagree. The Moral Majority contradicts itself by opposing abortion as murder while lobbying for the restoration of capital punishment for many crimes.' Bryan Green criticised Falwell and his followers for claiming to have 'a hot line to God for interpreting the Bible'. He also faulted the organisation for focussing on the 'small potatoes instead of the really big evils, such as racial discrimination, poverty and inadequate housing for the poor.'

Canon Green was never known for being too indirect! He was a master of the shock treatment, although he never purposely set out to shock people. He simply reacted to the moment. I was with him once in an Episcopalian Church in Northern California, which he perceived as being too syrupy and having a 'pie in the sky' vision of Christianity. He said from the pulpit: 'First of all, I want to thank the rector for inviting me. Second, I wish that I weren't here! (Laughter from the congregation) No, I'm quite serious. I wish that I weren't here. You have such a wonderful 'pie in the sky' version of Christianity that you really don't need me. You think that Christianity is one unbroken success story. Well, it isn't. Christ said from the cross: "My God, why hast thou forsaken me?" Christ, according to the scriptures was "a prophet without honor in his own country." So, as I say, you really don't need me. I might disturb you.'

Canon Green then proceeded to preach, and each member

of the large congregation seemed to be hanging on his every word. To repeat, Canon Green didn't go into the church intending to say what he did but, as the saying goes, the Lord moves in strange ways. One English writer once commented: 'Canon Green never likes to let the devil have all the best stunts.'

Here are some other examples of his spontaneity. Approximately four hundred persons went to an Episcopal Church in Berkeley, California one evening to hear Canon Green. Before the service started, he walked up the main aisle greeting a lot of parishioners and shaking their hands. Then, he announced in a loud voice: 'I'm just out here inspecting the sinners!' (Enormous laughter.)

Once, in a small parish, the organist in the back of the church started playing the organ near the end of the service, just as Canon Green was planning to say some final words. Green exclaimed: 'Stop the music!' The organist didn't hear and continued to play. Canon Green again shouted: 'Stop the music. Please tell the organist to stop!' The organ trailed off in dying tones. Green immediately said: 'Now, please don't blame the organist. It was my fault for not communicating with him properly. Now, you must not mind about a little incident like that. If you think that God minds about things like that, you just don't understand God. He minds about other things, but not things like that. Isn't this wonderful – this has given me an opportunity to make another mini-sermon!' There were countless examples of how Canon Green took an incident that might have been awkward or even numbing for most clergymen and used it to make a point.

As has been said about another outstanding clergyman, Bryan Green 'comforted the afflicted and afflicted the comfortable'.

Perhaps the theme that Bryan Green preached on most frequently during his university and parish visits in America was on the concept of Grace . . . that God loves us, no matter how undeserving we are of his love. He very frequently compared man's relationship to God to the love relationship: 'I have been married for more than sixty years and my wife, Win, loves me unconditionally – certainly not because I am deserving of that love. She loves me, with all my shortcomings and human failings. So it is with God's love.' Green once gave a brilliant series of four lectures on Grace called the Pyrtle lectures in Houston, Texas.

Another theme about which Canon Green spoke frequently in America – often in response to questions – related to 'a subject on which Christians frankly disagree – on whether only Christians go to heaven.' The Rev Charles Colwell, Rector of the Church of St Barrabas, Irvington-on-the-Hudson, New York, wrote his impressions of Bryan Green's speaking on this subject:

'In the fall of 1987, Bryan Green was leading a mission at a friend's parish in the Hudson Valley. I went, filled with many questions about a concept that I had been struggling with for several years – eternal hell. That evening, I was immediately struck by the vitality and, yes, the naughtiness of the man. He had an impish twinkle in his eyes. This elderly, white-haired preacher had a love and appreciation for his audience, which was a mixed group of professionals and blue-collar workers, of students, of wealthy and poor. The people hung on every word.

'Halfway through his address, Bryan took off his glasses, peered across the lectern and said: "Now, my friends, I want to talk to you about heaven and help you deal with all the rubbish about hell." My ears picked up as I listened intently for an answer to the disturbing questions I had been struggling with for years. Bryan quoted Origen who, in the third century, set forth a belief in what he called "universal reconciliation". "This makes sense to me," Bryan continued. "Great contemporary Christians also support this belief: William Temple, Robert Runcie and Hans Küng. In the end, I hope that God will save the worst of us and that hell will be empty. Otherwise, what a terrible defeat for God's love."

'Bryan quoted Origen again: "Jesus will stay on the cross as long as there is one sinner left." Bryan continued: "I came to understand a need for 'purgatory' about twenty years ago. When I face God in his love, everything will be known about me. Purgatory is the experience after death of the love of God face-to-face, where we will be judged by God's love and welcomed in. Dear friends, no one goes on God's garbage heap!" I had clarity at last.

This proved to be a momentous evening in my life.

'Bryan visited my parish three times in the following years, holding missions and meeting with clergy. He teased the dogmatic and challenged the liberal. Bryan Green deeply affected my life and ministry. I look forward to being with him again in the Kingdom of Heaven, twinkle and all.'

Bryan Green had a profound effect on many American clergy. There is, seemingly, an endless number of clergy who have said words such as the following: 'I would never have entered the ministry if I had not heard Canon Green when I was a student.' Or: 'he had a major impact on my ministry.' Further, he conducted many clergy conferences in the US on the practice of evangelism.

In student question-and-answer sessions, Canon Green often had to respond to the assertion that Christianity was a 'crutch' for those who were weak or who needed comfort. Bryan Green relished tackling that one! He was fond of telling the story of a woman friend of his in England with whom he had a friendly running debate over the years about Christianity. He met her once in his club in London for lunch, and she said: 'Bryan Green, I don't need your Christianity. I have found perfect peace of mind! I have found peace of mind by mixing some ethical philosophy and Buddhism and some humanistic thinking.' Then she sat back smugly with her arms folded, as if to say: 'What are you going to say about that!?'

Bryan Green surprised her by saying emphatically: 'Delighted to hear that you have found perfect peace of mind. Absolutely delighted to hear it! But I didn't know that Christianity had anything to do with peace of mind! Of course, in the deepest sense there is a real joy and a certitude but, actually, being a Christian is a very disturbing thing. There is such a gap between the way we are and the way we ought to behave, such a gap between the perfect example of Christ's life and what we see all around us, that it makes us want to shoot out in all directions doing things. Being a Christian in today's world is very disturbing indeed. But I am delighted to hear that you have found perfect peace of mind.'

Canon Green reported that when he left her, her peace of mind had been somewhat punctured. As he put it: 'I dropped her there. I'll pick her up the next time that I go through London!'

Canon Green frequently spoke to student groups on the subject of 'love, friendship and marriage'. Typical of such talks was one that he gave to five hundred Stanford students on the five questions one ought to ask before one thinks about marrying someone. The first question was: 'How long have you known each other?' Green said that one couple came to him, asking him to marry them, and he asked them how long they had known each other. They answered: 'a weekend'. He responded: 'Don't talk absolute bunkum with me! Come back in six months and I will think about marrying you!'

The second question was: 'Under what circumstances have you seen each other? Have you seen each other in bad times as well as good times? Have you seen the other person with friends and seen how he or she treats the parents? I even know some couples who only see each other having fun, and they can even argue about how to have fun.'

The third question was: 'What do you miss most when you are away from each other?' Sexual attraction is obviously important, but if that is the only thing that you miss, then you had better worry about your relationship.'

The fourth question was: 'Do you come from roughly similar backgrounds?' This is not an absolute necessity, but if my daughter were to marry someone from a different country, I would want her to live there for six months first and see how she felt about the culture.'

Bryan Green felt that the final question was the most important one: 'Do you trust each other?' He said: 'When I first knew that I loved Win, I asked her: "Do you love me?" She replied: "No".' He said to his audience: 'That surprised you, didn't it?' (Loud laughter.) Then he asked her: 'Do you trust me?' She replied: 'Yes, absolutely.' He said: 'Good, we'll start from there!' Bryan Green went on to say that of all the five questions, the one of trust was the most important. Without trust, there could be no deep, lasting relationship. A fair number of couples came to that lecture engaged or semi-engaged. Afterwards, there were reports of engagement rings being returned after the couples had heard Bryan Green's five questions!

To come full circle, Bryan Green's extraordinary forty-six-year ministry in America had a profound impact on the lives of hundreds of thousands. One is hard pressed to think of any foreign preacher who has had a deeper impact on American spiritual life. He was brilliant, witty, authentic, compelling, honest, dynamic, challenging, and much more. It could be said about Bryan Green what was said about another great teacher: 'One never knows where his influence stops. He affects eternity.'

Television sermon and interviews

The Bryan Green Society holds many unpublished tapes and sermons, some of which have been transcribed.

This section contains:

1953: Bryan Green preaching at St-Martin's-in-the-Bull Ring.

A sermon broadcast on ITV from St Martin's, Birmingham Parish Church, on Sunday morning 14 June 1970

Here in St Martin's are five people; you will see them presently.

They are all members of St Martin's. I shall tell their story exactly as they told it to me. One is a man looking for something, another is a man who was baptised. The third is a woman who was frightened. The fourth a man who came to see, and finally a woman who gave her life in service.

You will see them here in St Martin's and you will see what happened to them; and what happened to them will show you why I am not ashamed of the gospel of Christ which is the power of God unto salvation to everyone who believes. This is my topic this morning.

Before you see my witnesses I want to give my own personal witness. Forty years ago as a teenager I discovered for myself Jesus Christ as Lord and Saviour. Twenty-two years ago I became Rector of St Martin's. During all these years I have never been ashamed of Jesus Christ – I have never had any cause to be. I have often had to be ashamed of myself as a Christian. I have been ashamed sometimes of the Church of England, the formality of her services and her lack of enthusiasm. Ashamed sometimes of the way we Christians talk too easily about the Christian gospel – not making it plain that we have many questions and difficulties about our Christian faith. But let me say firmly once again I have never had any cause to be ashamed of the good news of Jesus Christ.

Why not? Simply because of Jesus Christ himself, that tremendous man who lived in Palestine nearly two thousand years ago, who died on the cross and, as we believe, conquered sin and death and who today is the Living Lord both of individuals and of society. He is the power of God in the very midst of us, although we often fail to recognise his Presence.

115

That the world is sick and in need of healing – salvation is the Bible word – cannot be doubted by anyone who has the eyes to see. Society itself is sick – look at the wars, bad race relationships, greed, avarice, exploitation, social injustice and all the rest. Look at individuals – look at yourself – see their frustrations, their anxieties, their fears, their sense of guilt, their deep loneliness often expressed by violent antagonism to others. The list is a long one. All of us know something about this sickness in our own individual lives and in the lives of our friends.

The dangerous fact is that often we don't recognise what is the cause of this pain that society and individuals are feeling. We know the pain but don't recognise the cause. Sometime ago my wife had a persistent pain. After a while I was able to persuade her to go to the doctor; she was X-rayed and it was discovered she had cancer. I am glad to say she has completely recovered after the necessary operation. But how dangerous it would have been if the pain had been allowed to continue and felt acutely, yet the cause had never been diagnosed. So it is with our society today.

What is the reason for this pain that grips the human race? It is because we are trying to live too much on what I may call a physical and mental plane. Today the sensual – I use the word in its proper meaning – the physical and material – is all important to modern man. The spiritual, the inward, is devalued. You notice the reaction sometimes: as when the Beatles seek mystical experience because they feel the need of something other than their material and physical success. Man is meant to be one whole person. His physical and sensual life should be linked up with and related properly to his inner and spiritual life. This shows to me man's deep need for God – because God the Living God is at the heart of life. If we have not got a oneness with God then, I believe, we cannot be complete and fully human persons.

This fact is exactly what the tremendous person Jesus made so clear. In the four portraits of him in the four Gospels he is obviously an amazingly fine man – a man just like us with all our difficulties, questions and temptation, yet giving his whole life in service to other people; healing, helping, teaching and finally giving his life in love; crucified by the world as it was in his day, just as love is crucified by the world of our day.

I have left out one important fact about Jesus. I notice that some of the modern plays about Jesus on television and elsewhere often leave out the same fact and so distort His image. He had a real oneness with His Father − as He said: 'I and my Father are one', and his life of prayer backed this statement up. His inward link with the Living God was deep and real; in fact so real was this relationship that we believe that in Jesus we see not only what man is meant to be like but catch also a glimpse, undistorted and clear, of what God at the heart of all life is like − the God of suffering love. 'He that hath seen me, said Jesus, hath seen the Father.'

This good news about Jesus Christ which can change men's lives and heal sick individual souls is also the power which can heal our sick society − indeed can heal right now someone who is listening to me − if we turn to Jesus Christ in faith and prayer, we enable the spirit of God to take hold of our lives and to bring healing and integration to us who so deeply need both. Christ does make a difference. Let me introduce you now to five witnesses in whose lives Jesus Christ has in fact made a difference.

The first four Witnesses were seen on the screen live from St Martin's while Canon Green spoke about them. During each piece a photo-caption came on the screen showing what each was doing because of commitment to Christ. This was not seen however in St Martin's.

My first witness is a man who was looking for something. Here he is. Fifteen years ago Ray came to St Martin's searching for an answer − his motive: how to find richness in life. As a boy he was forced to go to church regularly, several times on a Sunday. It put him off, though he still continued vaguely to believe in God. Deciding to become a teacher he went to an Anglican training college. While it taught him how to teach, it put him off the Anglican Church. When he came to teach in Birmingham he wandered round to various churches, still searching for this richness of life, which somehow or other he felt was linked up with God. So Ray came to St Martin's. One Sunday he heard a sermon on the words of Jesus: 'I am come that you might have life and that you might have it more abundantly.' That hit him! It was just what he was searching for. After that in his search he listened to the gospel as it was preached here and came regularly to worship.

Later on because of this link he began to help at the St Martin's Youth Centre in an under privileged area of this City. He helped with what is called the 'Penny Club', a weekly meeting for younger boys and girls, trying to share the little he knew of God's love by helping these children in their play and fun, by telling them stories and showing them how to be sensitive to each other and to other people. While doing this he discovered his own faith was being born within Him.

Today if he were standing here in this pulpit, Ray would say, and I quote his own words: 'I have much yet to learn of the richness of Christian living, but Jesus Christ adds a new dimension to life; Christ doesn't take away from life nor spoil it. He brings a richness to life, a richness which comes from a deeper understanding of God Himself.'

My second witness is Herbert who was baptised here in St Martin's some years ago. No easy thing to do in middle age, in public. What made him willing to do that? His wife, Anne, thought she ought to be confirmed together with her son, to keep him company. Here Herbert is with his wife. On the day of their confirmation, as she was waiting for the service to begin she naturally felt a little lonely. My wife was there, noticed this and spoke to her. From this contact they got to know each other, and Anne and her son began to come regularly to church bringing Herbert with them.

He was an interesting person for he had been brought up in a strict Free Church home. As he grew older he drifted away from the practice of religion and even from any convinced Christian belief. But he kept firmly to the moral and ethical standards which he had learnt as a boy. After the confirmation episode, as I said, Herbert began to come regularly to St Martin's. Some years later I was talking to him and asked whether he thought he was ready to be baptised. Herbert replied: 'I don't believe enough about the Christian faith.' We talked some more and then he said: 'Well I do understand that God loves me; this I can vaguely see because of Christ's death on the Cross.' 'That's good enough' I answered 'for baptism; after all that is what baptism is really about, allowing God's love to take hold of us.' So Herbert was baptised. The years passed; nobody pressed him to move into deeper commitment within the Christian Church. But one day he thought he was ready to be confirmed and so he was. Among the differences his commitment to Christ made, was that he offered to do some voluntary work for the Church in which he had found faith in Christ. Here in St Martin's we give to the church at home and overseas through a Regular Giving Plan and Covenant Scheme. As an accountant Herbert felt this was a job he could do to help, and as he said to me the other day: 'Looking back I think perhaps now I can call myself a Christian, though not a very good one.'

My third witness is a woman who was frightened. To see people dying can be a terrifying experience. As a young medical student doing her clinical work in the wards of a hospital for the first time, Stella discovered this. So frightening was it for her that she decided to give up being a medical student and take up a scholarship in a university studying physiology. Shortly after she arrived there, she fell in with a group of pleasant students, who happened to be Christians. They took her to their meetings. One day she heard the speaker talking about the Gospel of Jesus Christ. He appealed to her because he was so sincere and convinced; he message sounded sensible.

Her own religious background had been simple, formal church-going while at school, without any real, genuine, personal faith in the Living God. After she heard this speaker, faith didn't come to Stella straight away. But she did begin to think about the gospel of Christ, to read her Bible, seriously searching to find faith for herself. About this time she happened to come to St Martin's and fell in with St Martin's Under Thirty Group. She was still searching. What piqued her quite a bit was that other people came to her with their problems about boy friends and the rest, yet nobody seemed to help her with her problem, which was above all to find faith in the Living God. She finished at university. The obvious thing was to go back to medicine. This she has done and is practising now. Yet back again in the wards, Stella still had that inner fear of people dying and of death itself. In a kind of desperation she began to pray, to pray that God would become real. It was essential she knew to discover Him. As she prayed, gradually a conviction was born within her mind that Jesus Christ was indeed her Lord and Saviour. Her outward life didn't change very much, but that inner gnawing fear of seeing people die and of death itself disappeared, for in Jesus Christ, Stella had discovered a confidence both for life and life's responsibilities, and for death and what lies after.

The man who came to see is my fourth witness. Sometimes the gospel of Christ hits a person suddenly, dramatically and they discover that He has a message and meaning for their lives. It happened like this twenty-two years ago in St Martin's to a young man of twenty-five. Onslow first came out of curiosity to see a new rector and to hear what he had to say.

He had been through the war and if you had asked him then if he was a Christian, he would have said: 'Yes, I go to church quite often' and that is what he thought Christianity was all about. That Sunday morning, however, God spoke to him in the sermon. He realised that he, Onslow, personally had got to make a definite response to the claims of Jesus Christ. There was nothing dramatic about his conversion, except the suddenness of his discovery of the claims of Christ. He made his own response. Gradually his life began to change. Not so much outwardly but inwardly because Jesus Christ became more and more important to him.

As in every real conversion, Onslow began to see that part of living for Christ means being concerned for other people, because Christ is concerned for other people. About a year later, somebody said: 'Onslow, will you come and play the piano down at the Boys' Brigade Bible Class? They are short of a pianist.' He went down. Concerned to serve Christ by helping other people, gradually he realised he was dedicating his life to work with the Boys' Brigade. No easy task – for at that time the Boys' Brigade company was in an under-privileged areas, close to St Martin's Church in the Bull Ring. Yet those boys were God's children. Because of the friendship and help that Onslow gave them, linked with his faithful teaching of the gospel at the Sunday Bible Class, some of them whom you now see sitting in St Martin's have grown up to be officers, and in their turn have given their lives to Christ and are seeking to serve others in the ways open to them.

The fifth Witness was introduced by an empty pew in St Martin's seen live on the screen and held steadily till Margery Northcott's words were quoted. Then a photograph of her was seen on screen but not by those in church.

And now I come to my final witness. It is the witness of an empty pew this Sunday morning here in St Martin's, a seat which for twenty-one years nearly every Sunday was occupied by a very remarkable woman. I knew Margery well. For twenty-five years she had been my private secretary, first in London and then in Birmingham. Here is her story. Ten years before she came to work for me, as a girl of eighteen, she had won an open scholarship in classics to Oxford, a remarkable achievement for a girl in those days. But just before Margery went up to college she developed tuberculosis with severe haemorrhage. There followed for her not only the disappointment of giving up her studies but of spending many years – more than ten – in hospitals. Recovering a little she came to me as my secretary. Some years later another serious operation and she was left with only one lung.

The amazing thing about Margery was her courage, her friendliness and her faith. She never moaned, grumbled or talked about herself. She lived for other people and her service through her work. She got much pleasure out of life, for example learning to drive a car; and she gave much happiness to all her many friends. Then just before Christmas 1968 Margery was taken seriously ill and for some days her life hung in the balance; she recovered quite remarkably. Eighteen months later she died. During those intervening months a Laymen's Crusade was held in St Martin's and Margery was asked to give her witness to Christ. It was not the kind of invitation she sought, diffident and humble as she was, yet willingly she stood here in this very pulpit and told of her faith in Christ.

This is what Margery said. I quote her exact words as she spoke them herself from this pulpit. 'I had a happy childhood and schooldays. When I was eleven in response to the call of Christ, I gave my life to Him, and it is to Jesus Christ I try to look in all the circumstances of my life. When I became ill at the age of eighteen, my father had just died. With my illness I saw plans for a career disappear and a hoped-for marriage. Looking back over all the years since then, what I see is not so much the grief and disappointment and the heartache but rather the steadfast unfailing love of Jesus Christ as He gave me by His Spirit patience, hope and trust in Himself and in His purpose for me, together with a wonderful measure of healing.

'So it has been over the years and I can believe, because of Jesus Christ, that my life, ordinary and imperfect as it has been, has had a meaning and a purpose. I am sure that, when I asked Jesus Christ to show me what He wanted me to do with my life, He not only answered my prayers by leading me to the place of His choosing, but has had His hand on me in all its joys and opportunities, in all its difficulties and disappointments and He has used me in His service.

'Just after Christmas 1968 I knew the Doctors didn't expect me to live so I jotted down one or two messages for friends and at the end I said that if I did die, I hoped nobody would grieve for me overmuch because I felt that I could say with Paul that: "For me to live is Christ, to die is gain." Well I didn't die – so many people were praying for me to live. Now therefore I can say very humbly that Christ is my life and I believe that when my time comes to die, it will be the gain of seeing Him face to face.'

You have heard my five witnesses. They have told you what Jesus Christ really means to them. They are five ordinary people like you and me. They were not spectacularly changed yet they were different through accepting the good news of Christ. How? They found a new direction – to live for Christ. There came a real meaning and purpose of life.

Now what about you, you who are sharing this Service, have you discovered the answer to your inner sickness of mind and spirit in Jesus Christ? Have you got, as it were, a soul in your body, so that within you there is the power of the Living God to make you one whole person, living a meaningful and purposeful life, free from guilt and fear, with a sure hope for the future for yourself and for society? If not, will you ask Jesus Christ to give you faith in Him? Will you search for Him; will you pray with all your heart, asking Him to give you a work to do for Him, to take you and give you a soul, an inner faith bringing a personal relationship with the Living God Himself? Pray as you listen to the choir, asking God to take a human life and use it for His purpose.

> Thou hast a work for me to do: O Lord show it to me;
> Thou hast a place for me to fill; Give me grace to fill it to
> Thy Glory,
> Thou hast given me a soul to make; Make Thou it for me;
> And build me into Thy spiritual temple for Jesu's sake.
> Amen

Now a final word to each of you personally who have been sharing in this service with me. If you have been genuinely helped by hearing the gospel at this Service; if perhaps in your heart you have been drawn towards faith in God through Jesus Christ, maybe for the first time; if you are genuinely searching to find Him through prayer and to discover His love for you, wanting to have a deeper commitment or faith in Him, that He might meet your own personal problems, then I do invite you to write to me, Canon Bryan Green, St Martin's, Bull Ring, Birmingham. Write and tell me what you are discovering or want to discover through Jesus Christ and I will send you a booklet freely, which may be of help to you. So write to me if you want to. I should like to hear. The very act of writing may make more definite this witness of your genuine desire to find faith in God through Jesus Christ and to commit yourself to Him as Lord and Saviour.

So I end as I began trying to preach to gospel of Jesus Christ as I have tried to do however inadequately during my twenty-two years as Rector of Birmingham. Forty-five years ago tomorrow, 15 June, I preached my first sermon as a young curate in New Malden, Surrey. My text then came from today's second lesson: 'We proclaim Christ – yes, Christ nailed to the Cross'. Over the years since this, my experience convinces me that if Jesus Christ is offered simply and sincerely and plainly, then we can expect results – results of the Holy Spirit of Jesus entering people's lives and changing them. I invites you now to crown Christ today as the Lord of your heart and of your life.

The Motet *Thou hast a work for me to do* was sung unannounced and unaccompanied by the Choir — words by Dr W R Matthews lately Dean of St Paul's — music by R Walker Robson respectively one time Vicar and Organist at Christ Church, Crouch End where Canon Green held his first benefice.

A television interview with twenty American teenagers

Introduction
Life is a continual process of questioning and learning. We want to understand the why of things. We hunger for answers. It's through our deepest question that God is calling us to into the fullest possible knowledge of who we are and who God is.

We now join twenty American teenagers who have gathered together to share their questions on the Christian faith with British Evangelist and author Canon Bryan Green, himself a faithful questioner for over eighty years.

Canon Bryan Green:
The 'why' question is interesting – human beings have always been asking why. Science asks why – that's how we know all we know today – because we've asked why. Why is the universe? Why are we here? The man who knows the 'why' of life is able to bear nearly any 'how'; to face nearly any 'thing', so that's why we ask questions. But don't expect to get a clear answer about everything. All I can do is to try and help you – and myself – to think about a question that you put to me and find a way of approaching it. Now let's have the first question.

What makes Christianity different from other religions?
Of course in a slick answer I should say Jesus Christ – but that's too slick. What it's like is this. If religion, which I've explained is a link with God – being married to God if I may use that phrase without being blasphemous – then it matters a lot what we think of God, what we know of God, what God is like. And we Christians believe that in Jesus Christ we see a kind of God, a fuller picture of God than any other religion has. And the wonderful picture that Jesus Christ shows us of God is something no other religion has imagined, no other religion has got; it is that God really loves us and suffers for our sins because He loves us. He's

1969: a television interview in Ohio, USA. The gesture is typical: 'If you think about it logically, can you really believe that . . . ?

hurt by the way we behave, the way His world goes. Now, this idea of God who suffers because he loves us is an amazing discovery, because once you discover that God loves you like that, out of gratitude you want to love him back, and you ought to make your life different. It doesn't always happen like that but it should do, and that's why, when we know that God loves us and suffers for our sins and for the evil of the world, it isn't an escapist business, just going to heaven when I die, as a matter of fact it makes me want to engage evil. Put it like this, if there are tears in the eyes of God there'd better be tears in my eyes, and I'd better get to work to try and help His world to be what He wants it to be. And so that's what really makes Christianity different. It's the knowledge of what God's really like that Jesus Christ shows to us.

Everybody says that Jesus Christ died for our sins, but what does that mean?
When I was at college there were forty-nine different answers. But let me try and look at it in a simple way as far as I can. Have you noticed how people have stickers on their cars, and one of the most stupid stickers is 'God loves you'. How ridiculous can you be – why on earth should God love you, or me, just think what you are. There are about four thousand million people on this planet – it may be even more – and you're a speck, on a speck, in a vast universe. Now why on earth should God, the personal spirit behind all, love me? That's the big question. It's always been asked, and that's why Jesus Christ steps in. And I must turn to my Bible again for it says this, rather interestingly; I rather like this: 'God demonstrates His own love for us in this, that while we were yet sinners Christ died for us'. And as Christ died you mustn't think of an angry God in Heaven saying: 'I'd love to forgive those people on earth and show I love them, but I can't do it just like that; somebody must suffer'. So He sent His son, an innocent Jesus Christ, and he suffers bearing the penalty for our sins just like that. Now some Christians think that, and they're perfectly entitled to their views – please don't misunderstand me – but I can't buy that one, it doesn't make for justice. I cannot see how an innocent person suffering for another makes it possible for God to forgive my sins any more than they would in everyday life. But supposing God is in Jesus Christ; supposing that's an absolute

127

mystery, that in Jesus, as I've said before, we've got God present in the living humanness of Jesus, then on the cross God is suffering for my sins, the ordinary sins of his day – you know, I needn't go into them, the Pharisees, and heroin, all the lot, just like my sins; selfish, jealous, all the rest of them, all the evils of the world – he's suffering for them. He's bearing their consequences. The burden of our sins is on His shoulders, He's borne our sins on His own body on the tree. Now that makes sense; I can see how He loves me, marvellous love, He shares my sinning with me in my burdens and sins – how wonderful. He really loves me like that, does He really? I want to love Him back.'

Well, did Jesus die just to save Christians or for everybody?
Did Jesus Christ die to save Christians or everybody? Now I'd like to turn to the Bible because I do think we have to take the Bible seriously though some do look at it rather differently. But I want to read what the Bible says here: 'Jesus Christ is the atoning sacrifice', He died 'the atoning sacrifice for our sins, and not for ours only, but for the sins of the whole world.' In that very famous text, you remember, 'God so loved the world – the whole world – that he gave his only begotten son, that whosoever believes in him should not perish but that have everlasting life.' But that follows you see: if God is the God Jesus shows Him to be, a God of love who wants to bring us his children into a living relationship with himself, then he wouldn't die for some people and not for others – he'd no favourites. So God died for everybody, the whole world. What's the next question?

When Jesus was on the cross, what did He mean when He said: 'Father, why have you forsaken me?'
Now, I'm always interested in the way in which young people put their finger, so often rightly, on the important questions. Scholars completely differ about why Jesus said: 'My God, my God, why hast Thou forsaken me?' Some people say he was just semi-conscious, quoting Psalm 22, the burbling of a semi-conscious man. Other people say – I don't agree with this one – He'd lost His faith, as we can lose our faith. Of course, if He was really human, as well as divine, I won't rule that out, but I don't accept that one.

The other is that He experienced as human – and Jesus was, remember, truly man – He experienced complete rejection. His friends had left Him, His enemies had crucified Him and now it seems as if God didn't answer. He didn't get angry with God but He felt that God had left Him: 'Why have you left me, God, now when I need you most you aren't here?' It's an amazing cry but it says something to me – that nobody could ever go beyond what Jesus has gone. He really knows what it means to be utterly rejected by everybody. But it's a difficult question and there we must leave it I think. What's the next one?

Some religions believe that Jesus is the Son of God, and others believe that He's just a nice guy, but who's Jesus today?
Of course many people very greatly respect Jesus, like they respect Gandhi and others – Jesus more so – the great thing about modern life is people are still interested in Jesus; they can't get Him out of their hair, you know, He's got stuck with us, we've got stuck with Him. Jesus is a real mystery – something I can't explain. He was undoubtedly human, tried and tempted and ordinary like us – a real man, that's how his friends first knew Him. But as they knew Him better, and especially after the resurrection, they came to the conclusion that He was more than that. Here was God in some very special way, God behind all creation can easily do this I think. Showing himself in Christ in a unique and special way, so that as we look at Jesus Christ we're discovering God, and God's character and characteristics; as Jesus said: 'he that has seen me has seen the father'. And so Christians believe that Jesus was truly human – but He also was God himself, and we can see God in Jesus Christ in a very special way. And to give the reasons why Christians believe Jesus is truly man and truly God would take more time than we've got in this discussion but let me just make this one point. If you believe that God is not a person 'up there', a kind of entity running the whole show as a kind of autocratic dictator (which I don't and Christians don't); if you think God is a spirit with personal qualities behind all life, creating the world, the universe, still creating it – if God is doing it all the time, it isn't impossible to think that this creative spirit could emerge in history, in a unique and special way. So that Jesus is human and yet divine

at the same time. Don't think it's an impossible thing, but it is a mystery. And I'm not a bit surprised when a lot of Christians say: 'I can't take it, it's beyond me'. I often ask myself: 'Why am I a Christian? How can I believe it?' And yet I do, and for 2,000 years Christians have believed it and lived by it. And so that's really all I can say, and if you say who is He today, why Jesus Christ the living God, and when I know God in my heart, the spirit of God in my heart it's the living Christ, Jesus himself now present in my heart. So that's how we look at Jesus Christ today. What's the next question?

How can we have free will if God is all knowing and He knows everything that is going to happen?
First of all I don't really believe that God does know everything that is going to happen just like that. My wife, who has known me for fifty-six years, knows me pretty well, and she can pretty well tell you how I'm going to act. Now God who knows me very well, also knows pretty well how I'm going to act. But I don't believe He knows every single thing that is going to happen. Supposing I'm playing a game of chess with you and you're a world master chess player, you're going to win – but you want me to learn the game so you let me make my silly little moves. I occasionally make a good one by accident, mostly bad, you've always got the check-mate. No, God lets me make my little moves, I don't think he knows every single one of them, so my will is free but the total game is in his hands. I believe that's the right way of looking at God. Some Christians don't, they think God wills every single thing that happens. Well, if they do, they've got to live with the difficulties of that view – and there are many, if you believe God really knows everything I'm going to do. Where does my free will come in? Your point is good isn't it? I prefer the other one, where God's got the whole world in his hands but leaves me my little moves in between. So he allows me to sin, he allows me to go to war, he allows me to laugh, he allows me to be noble, so if I really move to do something good I can stand back and say – not with pride, but with humanity – I did that well. So I get a dignity, the dignity of being a responsible person. Making responsible choices.
I always wondered if there was an afterlife and, if there was, what it will be like?

130

Ever since human beings have existed apparently they've wanted to believe in an afterlife. Do you remember those lovely stories about the cavemen? When they buried their dead they often used to put food with them or even clothes with them and sometimes used to put weapons with them. So they pictured a life after death as being much like the life here – well, that's understandable. Man's always wished to live on after death. But that doesn't prove there is an afterlife, I must admit that. That great philosopher Bertrand Russell, who was an atheist, says that when we die we either rot or burn, and he has this awful phrase, all civilisation will end in the débris of a universe, we're all going to pieces there's nothing in it. Well, if you're an atheist that may be right. I can't prove there's an afterlife but as a Christian I do believe there is one, because Jesus, I believe, rose from the dead and in Christ we should all be made alive. So I believe that when I die with my body – and I'm eighty two and shall be dead before most of you, I expect – I shall be alive in another state, beyond time, because time's finished with. It's part of this world, beyond space but another way of living. Now, what that's going to be like I don't know. I don't picture pavements of gold and all that; I have to say it's like this – as Saint John puts it – when we die we shall be like Jesus Christ for we shall see him as he is. And if Jesus was a real man, then I believe in life after death. I shall be a real person, my realest self, my best fullest self – whatever that means. Whether I shall recognise those I love in heaven, I'm not sure, but I'm looking forward when the time comes. I don't want to die yet but when the time comes Christ, who loves me now, will take me through death to Himself. That's the Christian belief about afterlife.

Signs of a saint – tension and serenity

Introduction and questions by Ivan Bailey:
Hello. For me, serenity has always been the sign of a saint. And it came therefore as something as a shock when I was reading a book called Saints Alive by Canon Bryan Green to find that he said that tension was a mark of Christian character. Well, he's been a preacher across the world for over sixty years and he's here tonight to explain himself.

Canon Green, surely stress is a curse of modern society?
Indeed I should agree. Perhaps I'm wrong in using the word 'tension', but I did that provocatively to make you and other people think about what I meant. I think what I really meant to say was that, unless we're stretched, there's a stretching in our lives, we can't reach the depth of possibility in human living. It's something like a piece of elastic stretched between two nails, two fixed points.

But then surely one of those fixed points is a Christian serenity?
I agree, but there's another point and I'll come to it later. Yes, serenity indeed, and the peace of serenity is really a sense that God's love has a grip on the whole situation. That's an inner faith a Christian has – and non-Christians have got it – that God's got a grip of things. Now I remember once I had an aunt, she was a wonderful Christian, you might think she'd put people off but she never did – real saints don't. She'd talk biblical language, she was pious, she'd 'praise the Lord' and 'Hallelujah' just like that, you see. And one day she went to Paddington to catch a train to some engagement where she was speaking, and she got to the barrier, and the barrier was slammed in her face by the ticket collector, and she said quite naturally 'praise the Lord' and went off to get a cup of tea. When she came back the same ticket collector said to her:

'Excuse me, Madam, but what was it you said when I slammed the door in your face?' 'The barrier?' she said 'I can't remember.' He said 'Did you say "Praise the Lord"?' She said 'Yes, I did, because I'm sure God's got a purpose in my missing the train'. And he said: 'Well, madam, would you mind missing another train?' and she said 'Of course not'. And he said: 'I want to talk to you and I've got a tea break.' And he talked to her, and he was on the point of suicide, his marriage was breaking up, and she was able by missing that other train, to help him to give his life more fully to God, and in the end it straightened his marriage.

So in other words her serenity sorted out his stress?
Precisely.

Now that's an example of serenity, but what about the divine discontent at the other end?
Well that's the other end, that's the other point you see. And if there are tears in God's eyes there ought to be tears in our eyes, even if we can't do anything about it. I believe that to have a discontented conscience, a disturbed conscience, is part of being a Christian. I remember once I was doing some in-service training for the United States naval chaplains in America, and the Admiral gave me a marvellous dinner party. And as I went across to the buffet and filled my platter – I can't say plate; it was a platter, sirloin steak, beef all the rest of it you see – I came back to my place between two lovely ladies who'd got their platters. As I sat down I said, quite forgetting where I was – what I often do think I sometimes say out loud – I said: 'When I see all this food in front of me I can't help remembering that half the world is going to bed tonight feeling hungry.' 'Oh,' he said, 'don't spoil our meal by talking about that.' Now, you see I think it's wrong to try and paper over the cracks to push stress and starvation and suffering of other people under the carpet.

Would you say that's one thing about young people – good young people – these days, that they actually have this essence of?
I think that young people are often misunderstood. I'm deeply impressed at Wycombe Abbey Girls' School, where I'm a kind of

unofficial chaplain, with the concern the girls have for their friends who are unhappy, or lonely, or disturbed, or anxious about exams, they are very keen to help each other. I think we forget this and you notice the idealism when young people responded to that Bob Geldof, remarkable you know. It says a lot – you can't crush the idealism of young people altogether.

Where do you see this tension in the life of Jesus?
I think first of all He obviously was in touch with His father; I and my Abba – father – are one; I am that close to God. And yet he suffered in Gethsemane. He said I wish I didn't have to die and suffer. I'd have loved to miss the cup of suffering, but I must drink it if it's God's will. And he had to face this two-fold suffering.

Do you actually think that somewhere in the eternity there's a kind of tension in the mind of God when he looks round on the funny world of ours which is good and bad?
I have a feeling, if you really want to know, that God has a tension of frustration at the moment. I mean I must say if I were God I might look at this world and say: 'To hell with the lot of you. You're not fit to do anything with, you really aren't, the mess you're making of my world' – which is a lot of truth. And he doesn't do that, he holds his love.

What would you say is the distinction between worry in a Christian's life and tension?
Well, if you worry, you don't trust. If you trust then you won't worry – but you'll still be in tension.

So trust and tension can go hand in hand?
They can indeed.

Canon Bryan Green – thank you very much indeed.

A selection of Bryan Green's writings:

Bryan and Winifred Green about to welcome the Lord Mayor of Birmingham

Dealing with the Individual

This chapter from The Practice of Evangelism (Hodder & Stoughton 1956)
is reprinted with slight editorial clarification by kind permission of the publishers.

No task is more important or sacred than leading an individual soul into personal conversion. It is a subject which we must approach with the greatest diffidence, for the experience of conversion is the work of God's Holy Spirit, and His work with an individual personality is mysterious and unique. There is something abhorrent in this connection about any such word as 'technique'; even 'principles' is a term which must be carefully used. When we are dealing with real spiritual work we are moving in the realm of God's own working in the lives of men and women, and perhaps all that we are able to say is that we can observe that God normally works along particular lines. We must try to observe how He works and from this observation we can map out certain spiritual principles. Certainly such a careful analysis will above everything else reveal to us that God does move in mysterious ways, and that only in utter dependence upon His Spirit can we ever be used to lead a soul to Christ.

This ministry of reconciliation, of leading a soul into a restored relationship with God, is a very personal matter. It is said of the evangelist D L Moody that he was always eager for his sermon to the thousands to come to a close so that he might deal with the inquirers one by one in the after-instruction. His instinct was surely right. If then some seeker after God needs help from a Christian in order that he may discover conversion, then that task is for the Christian one of great privilege, and one which must be undertaken with the utmost care – and, in the best sense, diffidence.

Perhaps it must be emphasised – though no doubt it should be quite unnecessary – that we must keep in the fore-front of our minds the fact that each person we are seeking to help is a unique personality and cannot really be classified as a type or member of a class. We may have to group people for the purposes of clear thinking about different types of difficulty or of approach, but we must remind ourselves constantly that no person can be fitted neatly into a pigeon-hole. In any attempt to help we must seek to have patience and knowledge, thus making a determined attempt to get alongside them so that they will realise we are friends and are sharing with them, as it were, in the search for conversion.

Individuals will approach the Christian church for personal help for various reasons. How will the approach be made, and to whom? It may be the result of a casual conversation or chance association; it may be made to a person or to some lay Christian. The essence of the matter is that however the approach is initiated the person concerned wants help and is seeking it. To classify the help that is needed in general terms is exceedingly difficult, but we may perhaps single out four types, provided that we bear in mind that the lines cannot be too closely drawn.

Type 1: Human problems

There are many people who turn to the Christian with their human problems − a marriage is breaking up, a parent–child relationship is proving very difficult, a grievance is held against society, there is the inability to find a purpose for life. These problems are real problems and are deeply felt to be such by the people concerned; they must be helped with friendly Christian courtesy. It is our business to put our best endeavour into the attempt to help find a satisfactory answer. Every service chaplain or parish priest can amplify such instances from personal experience. It is quite likely that from our standpoint we know that what is really troubling the person is a wrong God-relationship and that only when they are right with ultimate Reality will they be able to handle rightly the particular problem; but Christian friendliness and courtesy demand that we do not say at the outset: 'If only you are right with God then your problem will be on the way to solution.' We have been approached with a definite request to deal with a specific problem; our friendliness and attempt to deal with it practically may open up for us in time the opportunity to point out the need for true conversion. If we are watchful we shall discover the possibility of showing that, unless the real self is

138

related to God in a living faith, the personal life as a whole will not be integrated.

One general warning is needed. We must not feel that we have failed our Lord because people who come to us with their problems often leave us without our having any chance of talking to them about God. We must not get a bad conscience because we have signed five or six forms in a morning and have not said anything about Christ to the people who brought the forms. We are not necessarily being unfaithful servants. In the first place we must never imagine that God cannot use us to draw someone to Himself unless we have spoken the word 'God' with our lips. And, secondly, we must remember that if we have shown charity and helpfulness, this may well pave the way for a future opportunity by creating confidence in the Christian church which we represent. Given this warning, I think it is true to say that, if we are watchful and prayerful, we may well discover that with experience we are given the knack – if that is the right word – of being able to get deeper with individuals, and to get deeper more quickly.

Type 2: In search of faith

There is a second group who come to us – people in search of faith; for one reason or another they have been driven to feel their need for faith in something or in someone, but that is as far as they have travelled. This today is becoming a more common attitude. The mess and evil of the world, and the bankruptcy of science to supply a right spirit with which to handle the situation, are driving men to look for a spiritual faith. Many are turning wistfully to the Christian church because they suspect that it may be faith in Christ that they need. They have little or no Christian background; they are very ignorant and do not really know for what they are looking. These people, of course, are not yet ready for conversion, but they are looking for teaching and guidance. What can we do to help such people?

We can lend them a book in order to clear away some of their ignorance about Christianity and to give them an intellectual grasp of the Christian faith. What I have in mind is not so much a pamphlet or tract (useful though these may be in certain

139

instances, but generally speaking they are too slight for inquirers at this stage); what they need is rather a simply-written book on the Christian faith in general, or giving the answer of Christianity to the particular difficulty that is theirs. It is better both for clergy and laypeople who lend books to have eight or nine carefully-selected ones which they themselves have read and know thoroughly. Lend the book then; but do not suggest that it should be returned to you by post. Say rather: 'When you have read the book, bring it back to me and I will lend you another.' This gives you an opening for your next conversation. You are able to find out what the seeker has discovered and what progress has been made. It is obvious that all of us who are wishing to help others will have different books that we shall lend; but it is worth while taking time and trouble to select the books and to prepare ourselves to use them.

Another way of helping a seeker is to suggest certain readings from the Bible, for so great is the modern illiteracy on spiritual matters that many who are seeking God and faith have not the least idea what Jesus Christ actually taught, what He was like as a person, and what He offers to do for the world. Do not make the mistake of saying simply: 'Read the Bible,' or you may discover that your friend starts at the beginning and tries to read right through, as happened once to someone I knew some years ago. Even in such extreme cases, absurd though it may appear on the surface, it is possible – and I have known it to be so – that when the seeker has been desperately in earnest to find God in Christ such a dogged approach to the Bible has been rewarded by the gift of God, for 'God is the rewards of them that diligently seek Him.' It is, of course, more reasonable to recommend a straightforward reading of the New Testament. I can recall an American student who came to some lectures I was giving on Basic Christianity in Kansas University. After the second lecture he greeted me: 'I enjoy listening to you and I am coming to all your lectures, but I don't believe a word you say.' Ten days later we happened to meet at breakfast, and this time he greeted me: 'Jesus Christ is either mad or else He is God.' 'What have you been doing?' I asked him. 'You have moved a bit since we last met.' 'Oh, nothing,' he replied, 'I was interested in what you were saying and so I have read the New Testament through three times.' 'You will be a Christian soon,' I retorted – and he was. These, however, in my opinion are exceptional cases.

Certain Bible passages and books are more suitable than others. In certain circles there is a marked preference for the Gospel of John. I can well understand the love a Christian has for this Gospel. Archbishop Temple tells us that he himself felt much more at home with John than with any other writer of the New Testament. But I am not convinced that John is the best book for the seeker first to read. It may well be Luke's Gospel that will help him more, and then perhaps parts of the Acts of the Apostles. We must also consider whether it is advisable to recommend that the reading should be in Moffatt's translations rather than in the Authorised Version. If we decide on the former it may be useful to recommend the new edition in which the chapters are laid out as in an ordinary book, without verse divisions. Anything we can do to remove strangeness from the reading of the Bible is valuable. There is no need to put any unnecessary stumbling-blocks in the way of someone who is seeking faith. I have on occasions felt it inadvisable to recommend the Bible itself, but rather a life of Christ which keeps close to the Bible text. It seems to me that at this stage what is required is not so much an exact knowledge of what the Bible says as a clear and accurate outline of the person of Jesus Christ and what He offers to do for us.

Some seekers are guided forward not by reading, but by introduction to a group of fellow-seekers. As in the mission field overseas, so in England, it is necessary today that in every parish clergy or laypeople should have a seminar or inquirers' group meeting regularly. Such groups should not meet continuously. Seekers should be gathered together for five or six or perhaps a few more meetings, it being understood that all the members are inquiring the way to faith, and exploring the pathway together. At the end of the period it is usually found that some have passed forward from seeking into faith; others do not at the time wish to pursue their quest; and the remaining few will be helped best by some other treatment.

Yet another method of dealing with seekers is to invite

them to come to church. In very many ways there is no better procedure than this – in fact, I would recommend that as a rule it should accompany any of the previous three methods. I say 'as a rule' because there are some people who would be put off by the utter strangeness and unfamiliarity of church worship so that it is best that they should not be asked to come. But for the majority of seekers there is nothing more helpful, provided that the local church is a live, worshipping fellowship. Here they can observe Christians praying and can pray themselves, as far as they are able to; here they can catch the atmosphere of worship and begin to realise the impact of the supernatural; here they can listen to God's Word and begin to understand the meaning of the gospel phrases. So unfamiliar have the ideas of Sion become to so many people that the first step must be to come once more within the sound of such ideas. It is rather similar to someone who cannot understand and appreciate Beethoven. When you begin to go to symphony concerts and try to listen carefully, you gradually gain some insight into the meaning of the music.

I have outlined four methods of helping the seeker, but there is one principle that underlies them all. We are, it is true, doing our best to clear up doubts and to answer questions; we are preparing the seeker for faith; but we must recognise that in a great number of cases intellectual difficulties are not the real cause of unfaith, but are only the rationalisation which people offer to themselves and to others of a deeper conflict or tension which has barred them from any vital touch with Reality. The true cause of this lack of faith in God lies in the moral sphere. The Rev Jack Winslow, speaking out of a large experience, categorically states: 'There are habits in a man's life which he detests but cannot break, or his conscience is burdened by past sins of which he is ashamed to speak; these things are coming between him and God. Prayer is impossible. God seems utterly remote. Reasons then spring easily to the mind to prove that God has no existence. In such cases no amount of reasoning will bring a man to faith. It is the deeper causes of unbelief which must be tackled.' (J C Winslow, *Reaching the Nine-Tenths*, p 8.)

That is why we must encourage the seeker to make an elementary experiment of faith. 'Look at yourself,' we may say 'if

God is real you know what you would like Him to do for you. If there are things in your life which a good God would hate, be willing to let them go. Now pray as best you can. Say to God: "O God, if you exist, this is what I am like. Help me to find You."' It is indeed amazing how a glimmer of light is given in response to such an honest self-surrender. In many cases it has been a real step on the way. Fulton Oursler, now a devout Roman Catholic and a writer of many religious best-sellers, tells how, searching for faith and desperate because he could not find it, he slipped into a church and prayed: 'In ten minutes or less I may change my mind. I may scoff at all this – and love error again. Pay no attention to me then; for this little time I am in my right mind and heart. This is my best. Take it and forget the rest; and, if You are really there, help me.' (Fulton Ourseler, Guideposts, September 1950.) As he prayed the answer began to come. The fact is that many of us who call ourselves Christians do not really believe that God can answer even while a seeker is yet seeking. If people are willing to give all that they know about themselves to all that they know up-to-date about God, then something is sure to happen. How can it be otherwise if we believe what Christ makes plain about the character of God?

Type 3: Christians seeking help

The third class of individuals who will come to us for help are Christian people who come for assistance in the Christian life. They are converted, but wish to make progress in sanctification. Here, on the whole, the clergy are better fitted to meet the need and are in fact to some extent meeting it. We shall be asked for advice about Bible reading, about church worship, about saying prayers, about overcoming particular temptations, about the positive attitudes that a Christian should take in the secular world, about guidance for life's vocation, and a range of similar problems. There are many good books on pastoralia and it is not my purpose to develop this subject in this chapter. I would, however, like to make these observations. There are beginners in the sanctified life who want help with meditation and prayer. I have found most helpful some advice which Dr Torrey once gave after a mission he had taken in Cambridge University. He urged the more mature

Christians to read the Bible and pray with a beginner once a week for several months. I took his advice to heart and have often arranged with young converts to meet them individually for fifteen minutes once a week for two or three months. I suggest that we take it in turns to read a few verses of the Bible together, choosing them for one epistle, which we read through during the period. The letter to the Philippians is a convenient one for this purpose. After we have read we each contribute our ideas about the passage and state what help or instruction it gives to us; then we kneel to pray. I begin, turning the words of the scripture into prayer, making a simple meditation. I encourage beginners to follow me in their own words. After two or three months I find that they have made real progress in the art of meditation and prayer, and can now stand on their own feet. No doubt many clergy will say they are far too busy to do this, to which I retort: 'Well, then, you must train your Christian laymen to do it, if you haven't time.' And I would add: 'It is worth while to make the effort to have fellowship with two or three beginners yourself, for I find that I learn quite as much as I teach.'

My other observation concerns the Sacrament of Penance. Christians who come to us for help in many cases are looking for cleansing from sin – not forgiveness in its initial sense of justification, but freedom from a bad conscience which they have as Christians. Here myself I believe that Catholic experience should guide us, and that the simple, formal method of confession followed by absolution is as valuable a method as can be devised. I know there are some clergy who prefer to get people to tell their sins privately to God and then to assure them of God's forgiveness. Others suggest an open sharing of the sins, and then together kneeling to seek forgiveness. I have not the least doubt that all these methods are used to bring peace to a Christian's troubled conscience, but there is a great deal to be said for the impersonal and formal method of confession and absolution – at least, for some people and on a particular occasion.

Type 4: Seeking conversion
The fourth group who come to us are those who are seeking conversion. They will not, of course, phrase their need like this,

144

but it is what they are seeking. They will probably say: 'I want God now,' 'I want to become a Christian,' 'How can I find the life that you have been preaching about?' 'I want what my friend has got.' They are seekers who have pursued the pathway towards Christ a certain distance, and they are ready for something decisive.

These people will come to us on many occasions. Here is someone coming quite casually; from out of the blue they have become aware of their need of God in Christ. Here are our confirmation candidates, for if our confirmation classes have been any good at all that is what many of them should want to know, after the period of instruction. It is the greatest opportunity of all to help young people and adults into conversion. I have often asked communicants about their confirmation preparation, and questioned them as to what the priest asked them during the personal interview. Very rarely did I gather that they were asked them, in effect: 'Have you found Christ? Have you discovered a new and living faith in God?' Almost always the question is slanted thus: 'Do you understand what I have taught you? Have you made a rule of life? Do you know about the Sacraments?' Look out for other opportunities to lead seekers to conversion. After a mission there will be many; after an ordinary service, if we keep our eyes open; at the time of marriage, or when visiting in a home.

This group of people who are ready for conversion (if we may describe them as such) are of real importance. In their lives spiritual processes have been at work through the Holy Spirit; they have moved along the pathway of pilgrimage; they are seeking the decisive moment when their faith in Christ may be certain and real in their experience. Unfortunately, it is just here that so many clergy and laypeople 'haven't a clue' as to how to help such people. In our theological colleges hardly any instruction is given in this important art, which we may call the psychology of soul-winning. Very few books have been written about it. A doctor faced with a patient who needs immediate help must do something, and must know what to do. The Christian faced with somebody who is at the point of sincerely and desperately wanting God as a living reality in his life must have something to say which will open the door into that experience. It is no good fobbing a seeker off by saying: 'Wait, God will come to you if you seek Him.

Go on saying your prayers, and perhaps you will discover what you are after.' Something more definite must be said, and I do not believe that we ought to stress the waiting. God does not mean, I feel sure, that people should go on and on and on seeking and never finding. 'Seek, and ye shall find' are the words of Jesus.

The Christian minister therefore must have some clear idea of the principles which should govern attempts to lead the seeker into the daylight of conversion. To avoid misunderstanding I want to make it perfectly clear that many people do come into a crisis conversion without any personal conversation or individual help from a Christian; in fact, there are many who would be hindered rather than helped by such intervention. Their spiritual conversion has been more after the fashion of a bud opening to the sun until the full flower appears. There is something very strengthening to one's own faith to observe men and women coming into the light of the knowledge of God through worship or preaching, through reading or friendship, without any direct and immediate help from another human being.

Nevertheless, there are those who do come to us and say in effect: 'I want to come to God, and I want to find Him now.' We must remember that at this moment we are touching something most sacred. Here I hope I may be forgiven if I give my own testimony. It is the most humbling experience that I know to lead a soul to Christ, or rather to be at hand when God finds a soul. Because I have been privileged to be an evangelist in the more technical sense of the word, I have been allowed to kneel beside some hundreds of people at the moment when God broke in to bring the light of His gospel, yet it is still to me as much a wonder as it was on the first occasion when as a boy of sixteen I was with a friend when Christ came into his life. That was thirty-four years ago, and I am still just as humbled and just as thrilled now when I see the knowledge of Christ come into men and women's lives and their eyes light up with the joy at the discovery that has become plain to them. It is to me as fresh as ever it was, and completely nothing to do with me. I suppose my own spiritual life has been watered and kept fresh more by such experience than by anything else – for it is here that I see God in action. If it is not the Holy Spirit of God dealing with the inner depths of their personality, then they may say they understand through the psychology you have used, but there is no light of the joy of understanding in Christ. One knows the difference between speaking that word of spiritual authority which unlocks that gateway of faith and using mere argument which produces only intellectual assent. When therefore these privileged moments come I am compelled to stand back and say: 'This is the Lord's doing, and marvellous in our eyes.' It is for this reason that I covet for every Christian, whether they be one of the clergy or of the laity, that from time to time they may have the privilege of being at hand when God breaks into someone's soul. It freshens, deepens and beautifies with an all-pervading warmth the whole of our ministry. It is something beyond compare with the opportunity of helping somebody in a personal human problem; beyond compare with helping a searcher to go on towards faith; beyond compare with helping a Christian in the life of sanctification. It seems to me to be akin to the privilege a mother has when she gives birth to her child; new life has come into the world. In the pain and travail of my trying to help a soul God has given new life; it is spiritual creativeness in its deepest and truest sense which no Christian ought to be denied. I am sure it is God's will for us all, and once we have had the joy of leading a soul to Christ we shall always be seeking further opportunities. Because it is the work of God and we recognise it as such we shall never be in danger of self-glorification. We shall never think that we know how to do it, or possess a technique. I hope we shall always tremble when we find ourselves confronted with a seeking soul. What we said so effectively yesterday will not do for to-day; unless God gives me the word to speak no real conversion will happen.

What then are the principles underlying God's work of conversion? There is one great secret, and perhaps it is the only one. It is to pray for a spiritual sensitiveness which enables one to see how God is leading a soul to Himself and then to seek to be an instrument to lead the soul a little further along the same path. God is trying to disclose Himself; reverently may I suggest that we should ask Him to use us to help forward what He is already doing. This precisely is the art of soul-winning. Again we are reminded of how completely humbling this fact must always be. We are dependent, utterly so, upon God. We want to co-operate with Him, and He is often willing that we should.

There are a few practical points in dealing with an individual that are quite obvious, but must be mentioned. We shall never help anybody unless we are free from hurry; we must give them a quiet, unhurried time. The over-busy parson is a real danger and menace. We should never be too busy to spend time with individuals. It is surely a prior claim in a parson's ministry, and, I should have said, in the life of any lay Christian. We must give the impression of complete leisureliness when talking with a person who needs our help. We must give our complete interest and attention. A friend once said about William Temple: 'He often only gave you twenty minutes, but he gave himself to you for the twenty minutes – and that was why he was able to help so many people, especially young men and women.'

This impression of leisureliness can be created by planning the time carefully. Use some common sense about it. If your visitor arrives at eleven o'clock and you know that you have another engagement at twelve, then you have got an hour for conversation. Do not start by saying: 'We have only got an hour.' Say rather: 'Now, sit down. There's no hurry; we have got an hour.' Then five minutes before the sixty minutes is up, if there is still more to be said and done, bring this particular talk to a conclusion, thus: 'We must stop in five minutes. We have got this clear, or that clear, haven't we? Now then shall we meet again? And in the meantime here are some things that you can do.' No doubt I am merely stating a platitude, but it of the first importance that we should never seem to be pushing people off, or hurrying them in their spiritual pilgrimage.

We ourselves can help by sitting relaxed, avoiding telephone interruptions, preventing others from coming in to disturb our conversation, using for this purpose a little 'Engaged' notice hanging outside the door. These little courtesies show a consideration for the person to whom we are talking, and surely are marks of Christian friendliness. Doctors behave like this out of professional etiquette; we surely can do the same out of Christian courtesy.

Once having sat down for the talk, come to the point

quickly. I hope you yourself will be a little self-conscious. I find that I always am when I am alone with one person who is in spiritual need, for the sense of responsibility is great. It is a very delicate affair to go deep down into another person's life that there in the depths of his being God may find him. The other person is probably more embarrassed than you are; therefore come to the point quickly. They do not want friendly conversation as an introduction, but to start right away with the business in hand. 'Why do you want to be a Christian?' 'What makes you want God?' 'How long have you wanted to find Christ? How have you gone about finding Him?' Questions of this nature are worth asking simply and sympathetically. The real purpose is to find out the background of the individual. Perhaps you have to start a little further back with some such question as: 'What can I do for you?' 'Why have you come to see me?' 'Tell me what it is you want to know?' We shall get all sorts of replies. 'My life's all wrong.' 'I want to be happy as So-and-so is happy.' 'I need a faith.' 'I want religion.' We can then develop this a little further by asking: 'Have you been to church?' 'Were you taught any religion when you were a child?' Or sometimes all we can suggest to open the conversation is quite simply: 'Well, tell me about yourself and your life, and any needs and difficulties you feel.' The purpose of this introduction is to try and get the person to whom we are talking to interpret themselves to themselves and to see the way in which God is trying to lead them into conversion.

Perhaps this is a convenient point at which to emphasise one fact which cannot be over-emphasised. All the time that we are talking or listening we must ourselves be in a spirit of prayer. Often when silence falls it is a chance to seek God's guidance – an invaluable chance. Sometimes we do not know what to say next; a deadlock seems to have arrived. Be honest; say something like this: 'I don't know what you think, but I feel that neither of us knows what to do next. I don't know what to say to you to help you to understand, but I do know one thing. If you really want God – and certainly God wants you – then He must be willing to show you the way to Himself. Let's take Him at His word and ask Him quite simply to show you the next step. We can do it as we sit here, silently.' Such moments of prayer are amazing in their power. Just the right word has often been given to me to speak, or something that I have said before which I now repeat, immediately brings spiritual enlightenment to the friend I am trying to help. In fact so utterly is this delicate task of soul winning the work of God's Spirit, demanding our complete obedience to Him, that it seems almost impertinent to go on to consider the four main principles underlying the experience of conversion, but go on I think we must.

Principle 1: Need

The first principle is that the soul must come to a real sense of need – to that point of despair when it is crying out: 'O God, I need Thee. Come to me and save me.' – for it is in the despair of the soul that faith is born. This is what is really meant by conviction of sin. It is when people discover that they are lost and helpless, utterly dependent upon God to rescue them. If there is no answer from Beyond, then nothing can help them. This conviction is much deeper than a mere sense of sins; it is rather a sense of sin, of sinnership. Sins are the fruit of which sin is the root. The Oxford Group did much splendid work, but I think sometimes they failed because the regular technique was to suggest that people should make a list of their failures against honest, purity, unselfishness and love; when the list was made these sins were surrendered. Instead of true conversion, the result was often only a psychological release, because sins had been, as it were, 'got off the chest'. We must not make the mistake of laying too much emphasis on sins, but rather point out sin for what it really is.

How can we do this? As a start we may well discuss the superficial or surface needs. It may be fear of death or of something else; it may be a deep sense of loneliness; it may be a weakness of will, wanting to do right but failure to achieve; it may be a sense of moral failure, with accompanying shame and guilt; it may be a lack of purpose in life, the aimlessness of living; it may be the very evil of the world, with a general sense of frustration and intellectual despair in the face of it. Whatever may be the superficial needs, it is our business to show that the real need is for God Himself. The great phrases here are of this kind: 'enemy of God, ungodly'; 'without strength, away from God.' It is the 'without God-ness' that is man's real need, and I want to press the point until the seeker realises that he must have God at all costs. It is only out of despair that he will cry: 'Unless Thou help me I must die; O bring Thy free salvation nigh, and take me as I am.' We must seek to let God use us as His instrument to bring the soul to the point where it says: 'I must have Christ or else I am utterly lost; I am hopeless without Him. Just as I am, Lord, take me – take me as I am.' So many temporary emotional experiences pass for real conversion just because people are not brought to this point of despair which is real conviction of sin. Never, therefore, hurry at this point of the interview. Far better send a person away again and again with the superficial sense of need unsatisfied until they come to the crucial point of understanding: 'I am without God and without hope. I must have God.' Conviction of sin, let me repeat, is conviction of sinnership; it is not just a conviction that one is rather a failure and has given place to some nasty sins in one's life. It is the conviction of a wrong relationship with God, of falling completely short of what man is meant to be. As Archbishop Temple put it: 'The alienation of man from God is a fact. It is our business not to deny it but to end it.' Our business in soul-winning is to end the alienation, or rather to be God's instrument that He may end the alienation; but first of all the soul must discover the reality of being alienated.

How can the soul discover this? We can explain, can simply explain, that the deep need is for God Himself. Point out that it is the I-ness of sin over against God; it is the I that rebels against God and won't have God in control. Such an explanation to the mature Christian may seem to be mere words, a merely familiar statement. It is amazing how, if the Holy Spirit is dealing with an individual, such words spoken by the Christian will have a spiritual authority carrying with it the power of conviction.

We can then use the Bible linked with our explanation; but we must know the Bible to be able to use it, and we must believe what the Bible says. The great Bible metaphors about man without God are 'lost,' 'dead,' 'blind.' If we believe the spiritual diagnosis that the Bible gives we can talk to people like this; the seeker says: 'I don't see what you are after.' I can reply: 'Why should you? You are as blind as a bat – the Bible says so. "The spirit of evil has blinded the mind of them that believe not." You must ask God to open your eyes.' Or perhaps the opening will be: 'I don't feel anything,' to which you can reply: 'How can you expect a dead person to feel anything? I never knew a corpse that felt anything. The Bible says that you are dead in trespasses and sins.' Turn to the Bible passages, point them out, read them together; then it will happen quite often that the seeker says quite helplessly: 'Well, what can I do then? I am hopeless.' You immediately reply: 'That is exactly what I am trying to tell you – without God you are' – and the Bible will have brought, through the Spirit, the conviction of sin.

There is, of course, the other method of using the Bible, by which we point to those passages which tell what the Christian life can be and what God does for those who trust Him. In the minds of seekers there is created a great desire to be what the Bible says we can be and they know they aren't; but how can they be unless God gives them the power? Here again the conviction of sin is beginning to come.

A possible method is that of challenge. It is a combination perhaps of the first two methods, but we should only use it if we find it comes naturally and spontaneously. 'Why won't God help me' asks someone. 'Why should He help you at all?' I reply. 'Why should He bother about you? You have never bothered about Him.' Such a challenge often illuminates the truth, and the seeker discovers that they have no claim upon God and their self-sufficiency is broken down. I remember an undergraduate coming to me and saying that he wanted to be a Christian. We talked for a while about his surface needs, and I said: 'Well, you are obviously self-centred and superficial. It is a kind of a vicious circle because the more you try to find God the more you concentrate upon yourself and your own efforts. I don't think,' I continued, 'it's any good talking any more. I can't help you and you certainly can't help yourself, so we had better say good-bye.' As I showed him across the room and out of the front door he kept protesting that he wanted to find faith and couldn't I help him? As he went out I called after him: 'You can't do anything; I can't do anything; but God may be able to do something.' When he got home that brought him to his knees in real conviction of sin.

Principle 2: Offering

The second principle is to present the offer of Christ to the person who has come to realise a sense of need. This offer is best given from the gospel story either by some definite passage of scripture or by some story of how Christ met the need of an individual. Here the particular art is to make the offer of Christ correspond with the superficial need the seeker has admitted. We can show in this way that God meets our need of Him, but that He meets it at the point where we most realise our need. If the superficial trouble was loneliness, let the friendship meet that; if it was moral weakness let the power of the living Christ deal with that; if it was a sense of guilt, then the forgiving love of Christ can bring God's peace. We must never bring the offer of Christ to bear on people until they have discovered a sense of basic need. Far better send a person away with the words: 'I am afraid we can't get any further at the moment. If you don't see that you need God the offer of Christ will have no meaning.' Where there is a realised need the offer of Christ will become luminous and personal; the soul realises that it is God's answer for himself.

We must not worry about giving a completely balanced presentation of the offer of Christ. At that moment we must not try to present the whole story of Christ's offer. If once a person has come to accept the offer of God in Christ at the point of his conscious need, after their conversion they will realise how much fuller is the complete gospel offer. Bunyan made that perfectly clear when Pilgrim entered the wicket gate and found the way of life. His conscious need was chiefly how to escape from the City of Destruction; only later did the burden roll off at the foot of the Cross. Or to put it another way, let Christ in His fullness be represented by a circle; He touches the soul at the tangent of its need; but if the soul gets on the circle of Christ by identification with him it will not be very long before the soul passes round the whole circle and all the glory of Christ begins to take on meaning.

Principle 3: Faith

The third principle is the act of faith. Given a sense of need, confronted with the offer of Christ, the soul must make a response. The response is the act of faith – the simple acceptance of what God is offering in Christ. It is an act of will based upon the truth the soul is beginning to see. Repentance is the negative side of faith. If I am offered a box of chocolates and my hands are full of stones I drop the stones that I may receive the chocolates. Repentance is the willingness to let drop out of life all that hinders God, that in faith we may receive what God in Christ waits to give. (See note on Repentance at the end of this chapter.) There is no need to stress the idea of penitence and conscious sorrow. This often follows after conversion when the goodness of God and the heinousness of sinning are more truly perceived. If the soul is willing he can receive the new life in Christ. 'The wages of sin is death, but the gift of God is eternal life through Jesus Christ.'

We must watch our words carefully. Avoid using the word 'do'. Faith is the acceptance of a gift of God is waiting to bestow. The pride of the human heart is always on the alert to raise its head again by some act of self-effort. Our business is to persuade the soul to cease its deadly doing and simply to receive. A useful illustration is that of a heavily-laden train in the station, with its powerful engine ready to take it on its journey. The coupling link joins together the need of the train and the power of the engine. Faith links my need with God's power. We must not suggest that there is any value or merit in faith. It is simply our trust in God to meet our utter need. 'By grace are ye saved through faith.'

How can we lead a person into this act of faith? From one point of view we may well ask can there possibly be a way or a technique? Surely it is quite sufficient for a soul in desperate need, under deep conviction of sin, to whom Christ has been offered to be told: 'Now trust Him,' and surely seekers will come to God as best they can? In fact, may not the act of faith be almost unconscious and be rather an insight that dawns upon the seeker even as Christ is being offered? Will a seeker not grasp at the gospel as a drowning man grasps at a straw, and believe unto salvation. I am convinced that time and time again this is what does in fact happen and that the eyes of the soul are opened – and we see, believing.

On the other hand, experience shows that many people find it necessary to have a focus for their faith. Personally I tend to use a passage of scripture – there are many that are suitable. For example, we can turn to: 'Come unto Me, all ye that labour and are heavy laden, and I will give you rest.' 'How much more shall your Heavenly Father give the Holy Spirit to them that ask Him?' 'They that cometh to Me I will in no wise cast out.' 'Behold I stand at the door and knock; if anyone hear my voice and open the door I will come in' – and many others. Consider one method of using: 'behold I stand at the door and knock; if any man hear my voice and open the door I will come in.' I like to point to the passage in my New Testament and then explain its message. God takes the initiative and approaches the soul in its need. Hearing His voice means, as a little girl once explained: 'to feel wrong inside and as if you want Jesus.' The opening of the door is the act of the will which trusts God in Christ to take control. 'Suppose,' I suggest, 'I own a room, but keep it filthily dirty and untidy, with broken furniture about the place; supposing you love me and knock at the door, offering to enter and help put things straight. How would I let you in? Surely I should say: "Come in, please; turn out the broken furniture and help me tidy up." So with Christ; ask Him to enter you life; say to Him: "I am yours. Come in, turn out the broken furniture of bad habits, take away the pictures and put up on the walls of my imagination pictures of Christian standards; clear up the dust and sweep away the filth." That is what the act of faith in Christ means. That is how we open the door.' I then go on to explain very carefully that Christ has promised to come, if we will open the door and receive Him. And faith rests on His promise and not on our feelings.

What happens next? There is a good deal to be said for sending seekers away to do their own business alone with God. This is not a time for any other person to obtrude. There is, however, a practical difficulty. For many people there is not the opportunity to be quiet and alone. Besides, our Lord made it so clear in His parable of the sower that 'when the seed is sown then cometh the devil.' The pressures of the secular and the material are tremendous, and the still small voice can be so easily drowned by the noises of daily life. That is why it is often wiser to suggest that the seeker should make a response of faith to Christ immediately and in another's presence. If this is what I decide to be best I say: 'Let's kneel down together that you may put your trust in Christ.'

It is very rarely that I ask seekers to pray out loud. I want them to forget me at this sacred moment and to talk to God alone. Rather do I tell them that I want them to be alone with God and to open their lives to Christ. I simply say: 'Just tell me when you have finished praying.' Then we are silent. I pray while they are praying. After a while they indicate that they have finished praying. Immediately I ask: 'Has Christ really come to you?' or: 'Has God made Himself real to you?' or: 'Has He met your need?' If it is the work of the Holy Spirit and a real act of faith has been made, the answer is almost invariably something like: 'Yes, I think so.' My next question is equally important: 'How do you know?' As I have tried to explain so carefully a few moments before that we must trust the promise of Christ, and that it is not any feelings but what Christ says that matters, one would expect the answer to be something like: 'Because Christ promised to come.' Invariably the answer is quite different on these lines: 'Because I feel it,' or 'I know it.' In other words it is an experience that has come, an inward realisation of Christ's presence that has been given. I always answer: 'I am glad to hear it. Thank Him out loud.' The instant response is a simple act of witness in a few words of thanksgiving. The simple words are very often only: 'Thank you, Lord Jesus, for coming to me.' At this point I pray. I do not say: 'Lord, I thank Thee that he has let Thee into his life and that Thou has become his Saviour and Lord. Please show him what to do next and help him to read the Bible, to say his prayers and to go to church; help him to make resolutions at the very moment when grace has acted in response to faith. No, the kind of prayer that will help at this stage is something very simple: 'Lord, I thank You that You have come into his life and become his Saviour and Friend. Help him to keep his eyes open to see what You tell him to do next, that he may know that You are leading him and may learn to trust You better. Amen.' The act of faith must pass into the attitude of faith. 'As many as are led by the Spirit of God, they are the sons of God.'

Principle 4: Assurance
There is the fourth and last principle of which we must take note of. We are meant to have the certainty of assurance. In the New Testament we are offered not only a personal relationship with God

in Christ, but the certainty of that personal relationship whereby we can cry with confidence: 'Abba, Father.' This assurance is not concerned with our feelings or passing emotions. It is a conviction of faith based upon the very character of God. Saving faith is not saying as it were: 'Please, God, come into my life': It is saying: 'Thank you, God, because you have come.' We must point out to new converts that we are not asking them to believe in a few words printed in ink on a piece of India paper. Behind those words: 'If anyone hear my voice and open the door I will come in,' stands the whole act of God in Christ which guarantees His character, guarantees that He is a God who has come down to deliver. We must point out something of the meaning of the death of Christ on the Cross – Christ, who gave Himself for people who did not want Him and tried to put Him out of their lives upon a cross. Behind those words: 'I will come in,' stands the Person who said them – God in Christ, Who pledges Himself in the death on the Cross to give Himself to all sinners who will receive Him.

In this way we try to ensure that the new convert's faith rests on God and on His character alone. We do not need a faith which rests on anything more than the character of God, and if it rests on anything less it will not suffice. It must rest where it only should rest, in God Himself. Human pride has been broken and the new convert can take no pride in his feelings, no pride in a resolution, no pride in a changed life; it is trusting in a promise, and it is impossible to have pride in a promise which is based on the character of somebody else's love. The experience is in fact: 'Nothing in my hand I bring; simply to Thy Cross I cling.'

There is one final point that I must make clear. I am not suggesting for a moment that the procedure I have outlined, with its four principles, is a pattern slavishly to be followed. God deals with the human soul in a variety of ways. All that I am trying to emphasise is simply that when we analyse the movements of a soul in conversion these four principles seem to operate. I have separated them out for the purpose of clear analysis, but in the actual event they may not be clearly defined. I have no intention of stereotyping the approach of God to an individual and that individual's response to God's approach; and this applies both to the gradual, almost unconscious conversion as well as to the crisis conversion which we have been specially considering; it applies equally to the person who comes into conversion alone through some unexpected means, and to the person who seeks out help from a Christian.

In this chapter we have been considering what we are to say to a seeker who comes to us desiring to find God. We tried to show the need and put before them the offer of Christ. They leave us believing in God, in God Himself – in God because of what He is. The conversion and assurance are anchored in the love of God and in nothing less. This is the object of all soul-winning.

Note on Repentance

The biblical context sees the individual as a person-in-a-relationship. The person is in relationship with sinful humanity, of which they are inescapably part. They are saved into the Body of Christ when they find themselves in right relationship with God and their fellows. God deals with us as children, that is, as differentiated personalities, but He does not deal with us in isolation from our fellows.

It is for this reason that the barrier to faith at the time of conversion is often an unwillingness to get right with our fellows. It is not, of course, that by putting ourselves right with others we are therefore putting ourselves right with God, or, worse still, can think that we earn His forgiveness; it is rather that, because an individual is a person in relationship with others inescapably, we must be willing to be in right relationship with others – which is the only real situation for us. Thus only can we find ourselves in a position to be put right with God – Who is Reality.

This basic idea should guide us when dealing with seekers at the point when they are ready to make an act of faith. It may well be that they find they cannot accept the offer of Christ because of a barrier. This barrier may turn out to be an unwillingness to put right some wrong human relationship. We must not say: 'You cannot make an act of faith and accept Christ as Saviour and Lord until you have put yourself right with your fellow.' Rather we should say: 'If you are willing to straighten out the relationship, then that is what God wants at this moment.' This is important, because repentance is not a change of mind

158

which puts us right, so much as a change of mind which makes us willing to be put right. To alter the wrong human relationship at this moment may well seem to be beyond the power of the seeker. If, however, seekers are willing to be put right they can then make the act of faith, and discover Christ as Saviour. After conversion the power of the new life will enable them to alter the relationships which they are willing should be altered.

We need not list such wrong relationships. A few illustrations will be sufficient. A young woman seeking Christ could find no peace and assurance. The barrier was a theft she had committed in a house where she was working. 'It's five miles off,' she cried, 'and it's too late to go tonight.' I pointed out that God wanted at that moment her willingness to restore the stolen property, not the act of restoration. She was willing, and immediately able to believe. Next day, in the power of her conversion she was able to make the restitution.

I remember a man alienated from and antagonistic to the Christian Church because of his contact with a certain group of Christians. He wanted Christ, but was unwilling to accept the Church. When he saw that he must be willing to accept the fact that after his conversion he would still not be perfect, just as the Church itself is not perfect, he was able to discover the peace of God, and shortly afterwards to find his place within the Christian Church.

A middle-aged woman on the point of conversion suddenly said: 'But I won't forgive my sister; for twenty-five years we haven't spoken.' Until she was willing to forgive, God's forgiveness could not be given to her. But it is important to notice: 'until she was willing' and not 'until she felt forgiving'.

The same principle is important when dealing, for instance, with alcoholics. The barrier to faith in their case is often the sense of utter impotence to get rid of the habit. How then can they become true Christians? Only when they see that by letting themselves go to Christ as they are, willing to be delivered, can Christ come to them. After their conversion the power to overcome the habit will be theirs.

159

January 1991: Bryan Green's 90th birthday.

Is religion really important?

Woman 1976

A ten-year old schoolboy once asked me a question that went straight to the point: 'Why is there religion at all?' Well, is religion really important – or is it simply a matter of taste, like what to have for breakfast?

My short answer is that, without religion, I do not believe men and women can be proper human beings. For a vital difference between animals and ourselves is that we have a religious instinct.

This has always been a mark of human beings. Even among primitive peoples there are forms of religious belief and practice: so far as I know, anthropologists have never discovered an atheist tribe.

Of course people have made many mistakes in seeking for God: they have often got Him wrong and attributed to Him some of their own base passions and failings. Sometimes people's religious beliefs and practices have made them narrow and intolerant of those who do not share their views. But very often religion has shaped the culture of tribes and nations, inspired individuals to sainthood and martyrdom and prompted people to serve others.

False religion that is mere nominal believing can be the opiate of the people, but true religion, which is based on the living faith and an all-powerful God, can be the mainspring of human action and a source of deep human happiness.

O Lord, happy is the man who trusts in thee – Psalms 84:12.

What is the Christian belief?

Woman

A college student asks me a most reasonable and important question but one to which it is difficult to do justice in a short article. 'I would like to know what are the basic beliefs of a Christian. This may seem obvious, but I have never been told, and I would like to know whether I can honestly call myself one or not.'

161

First of all, Christians share some convictions with others. They believe behind all life and at the heart of it there is a living God – one living God. It is this personal Power who is Creator of all and the inner life within everything that is.

They believe that humans are, so far, the highest creation of the mind of God, the crown of the evolutionary process. All are brothers and sisters – the children of one common Father.

And now here is the particular Christian conviction. It is, to use the Bible phrase, that 'Jesus Christ is Lord.' This means not only that Jesus was the best man who ever lived, more truly human than anyone else, but that in and through Him we can see what God is like.

I want to stress this point: what enables people to call themselves Christians is not that they are born in a nominally Christian country, or have been christened, or are nominal members of a church: and it is not simply believing a certain number of intellectual propositions: people are Christians in the New Testament sense when they are able to say with sincerity: 'Jesus Christ is Lord of my life.'

Christianity is not a philosophy but a personal relationship with God: it is not a creed accepted with the mind: it is the living Christ to whom I give obedience and through whose spirit within me I seek to serve others.

Reading what I have written I realise how inadequate words are to answer the student's question. But what I have said is what I believe any understanding Christian would have said from the first disciples right down until the present day.

If, like the student who wrote to me, one has not this conviction and experience, one is not necessarily an atheist or agnostic: it is possible to be a believer in another religion or a genuine seeker after truth, but one cannot in all honesty say that one is a Christian.

That Christ may dwell in your hearts by faith – Ephesians 3:14–21.

The best of friends
Woman

'Christ is risen!' The Eastern Orthodox church has a lovely custom. On the Saturday before Easter the churches are thronged late at night with worshippers. The building is in complete darkness. Immediately after midnight, on Easter morning, there is a blaze of light and these words of triumph ring out on the lips of thousands.

They are remembering how Jesus Christ, who died and was buried, rose again in triumph on the morning of the third day. Exactly what happened is not clear. Even his disciples were uncertain about the sequence of events, but on one point they were unanimous: the one whose body they had laid in a tomb had now appeared to them – at different times – alive and victorious over death. True, his body was in some way different. They saw him and then he vanished. This is the account the New Testament writers give with convincing genuineness.

On Easter Sunday when countless Christians throughout the world proclaim 'Christ is risen!' they think first of that happening long ago: but then they express their joy that the living Christ is still with them.

It is this continuing personal relationship with the living Lord which lies right at the heart of a true Christian faith and life. None of us can escape from moments when, from a human point of view, we know we stand alone. The most sympathetic friend, for instance, cannot fully share with us some great sorrow.

Most Christians would want to say that in moments like these they know the tremendous strength that comes from believing in the presence of Christ.

But it is not only in the times of our weakness that the conviction that Christ lives matters. As we seek to serve others and adventure into life with purpose, we often feel that our own resources are not enough. Then we open ourselves to the power of that living Presence and discover an inner strength to face what we cannot do alone. There is more to the Easter message; but for Christians courage and strength spring from the truth that 'Christ is risen!'

To know Him and the power of His resurrection – Philippians 3:10.

Let's make it last

Woman 1961

Wintry bitterness too easily replaces the tenderness of Christmas.

What is the fascination of Christmas? Each year it puts its grip upon us all, and brings out the best in most of us. Even old Scrooge could not resist the spirit of the festival, and had to succumb in the end to its power. Happiness and good will dominate for a time.

I suppose the fascination comes from a number of facts. It is a holiday season. It is a time of family reunions, greetings, gifts. Above all, perhaps, it is the children's festival, and their joy infects us all, making some of us feel young again.

Carols play their part. People who never go to church will go to a carol service. Agnostic students at a university will join a carol party, and sing as lustily as any. Factory workers in a canteen will join without embarrassment in the familiar words.

The picture of the Mother and Child has an appeal for many who may normally have no use for religion – somehow this image says something to their minds. I suppose it is because deep within us all we know that this is one of the greatest of all human relationships. Whatever our age we are still children at heart; we need security, love, someone to depend on, to share our joys and sorrows.

Whatever our own experience during childhood may have been, instinctively we know what a mother ought to be, and if we have been fortunate we have experienced what she can be in a family.

Here then in the picture of the Mother and Child we see the true relationship which we all need, and while the Christmas season lasts the idea sweetens our own relationship with other people.

What a pity the good will and the peaceful friendliness do not last. Sometimes they do, but not nearly often enough. Too soon we pass from the spirit of Christmas to the bleakness of January and the winter winds of March. Bleak selfishness and wintry bitterness so easily replace the tenderness and good will of the Christmas season.

It need not happen like this, as many know; for after the

child of Christmas was born He did not just die. He lives, and His Spirit can take hold of our spirits, and make in our hearts a continuing Christmas festival of peace and good will. This is what we ought to mean when we talk of the joy of Christmas.

The Bible has something to say; see Luke 2:1–20.

A gift from God
Woman

Here in St Martin's we are in the centre of the city of Birmingham. On a New Year's Eve hundreds of people throng the streets, dance in halls and pubs. Then at a few minutes before midnight we hold the Watch Night Service. It is a strange and varied crowd that enters St Martin's. Some have been drinking a bit too much; others come simply out of conventional custom; but it's a crowd all right.

I am glad they all come. Maybe it is a bit sentimental; maybe the emotions are only for the moment, the moment when the clock strikes twelve, and afterwards their lives go on very much the same as they did before. Still, I am glad they are there.

In a church that stands where a church has stood for over seven hundred years, in a house which is the House of God, made His House not by the words of a bishop but by the prayers of thousands of people who during the centuries have met there, it is completely impossible to escape the sense of the presence of God.

Can you doubt that God can touch a life in a moment and make it quite different? In a moment when the clock strikes twelve we can gain an entirely new insight into the love of God and know then that our past has been forgiven. In a moment, like Paul, others can find a new Master for their lives and their selfish desires can then be dethroned.

In a moment a woman burdened with sorrow and self-pity can meet a Friend and go out into the new year knowing that no longer will she have to bear all her burdens alone.

It is the glory of the Christian religion that the invitation of Christ can be accepted and change our lives, giving us new hope and new strength for whatever the future holds.

Come unto me . . . and I will give you rest — Matthew 11,25–30.

Red letter day . . .

Woman 10 October 1964

'Good news' can mean different things to different people – a happiness received, or a happiness to give.

'It was one of the most welcome letters I've ever had.' As my friend said this, my wife and I were sitting having tea with her in her home and I realised what a remarkable woman she was.

In her middle fifties, she has suffered from acute rheumatoid arthritis for twenty-three years. The illness started during the bombing of Birmingham during the war.

In spite of great physical incapacity of hands and legs, she has kept her home beautifully neat and clean. Her radiant spirit has made it a genuinely happy place. Her daughter's teenage friends enjoy going there and meeting her, and her older friends leave the better for their visits. Here is a real triumph of the human spirit over physical illness.

What made it a red letter day for her would not have been my choice. It was, in fact, a communication from the consultant of the new Rheumatism Research Clinic saying that her request to become a 'guinea pig' had been accepted.

Since last Christmas she had been into the clinic several times, and she had countless injections and two operations.

Her comment is simply this: 'I am used to all these injections and I help the doctors all I can.' She is genuinely finding much happiness in offering herself for experiments in order that new discoveries in medicine may be made.

Today there is much that is selfish in our national life, but there are also many people who are seeking to give service to others – voluntary helpers in youth clubs for instance, women who organise the 'Meals on Wheels' service, the neighbour who helps someone next door when she is ill – and many, many others who give simple acts of service.

There are many teenagers too, who give service to the community. The best kind of service is very often that which is unnoticed and removed from the public eye – as with this friend of mine and some schoolboys who regularly visit a handicapped and lonely man – and is quietly and unobtrusively given day after day, and week after week.

Jesus praised this kind of service and pointed out that such people will have their reward, for as He put it: 'Your Father which seeth in secret shall reward you openly.' The happiness that others notice is often the result of secret and private service.

I wondered at the courage of my friend in facing the experiments. Quietly she gave me the secret: 'I don't care who knows about it. I always pray about these things, and I don't mind.'

As you did it to one of these my brethren you did it to me
— Matthew 25:40 (Revised Standard Version)

A matter of conscience
Woman 1961

To honour one's parents is a binding commandment – but parents, too, have obligations.

She wrote to me: 'My parents don't want me to marry him. They don't think he is suitable, largely because he hasn't the same background as I have. Do you think I ought to follow my parents' wishes, or not?'

Perhaps this question seems more suitable for a marriage guidance column than for answer by a parson in a religious article. But as I read on the letter made it plain why the girl had written to me.

It was for her a matter of conscience. In her own way she had a faith in God, and was trying to be a Christian. Ought she then to follow the teaching of the Bible and obey her parents and give Michael up, or would she be right in obeying her own desires and marrying him?

As in so many similar questions, things are mixed up. Partly, Mary needs advice about Michael's suitability – that is a marriage guidance question. Does she really love him or not? Does he love her enough? Enough to make up in a deep personal relationship for any differences in background and culture.

But besides this there is the moral question – and I am glad that Mary recognises there is a moral question. So often young people seem to feel they can ignore their parents, dismissing them as old-fashioned and not understanding – besides, young people claim: 'We are independent now and our parents' wishes no longer matter.'

The Bible doesn't teach this, and I believe the Bible is right. 'Honour thy father and mother' is a binding commandment, and being twenty-one doesn't entitle anyone to break it. The deep natural relationship between parent and child is an abiding relationship, and God means it to be so. It is wrong when we try to disregard this relationship and ignore our parents' wishes and desires.

But the Bible is equally clear that parents have a responsibility. There is a clear command to all parents: 'Provoke not your children to wrath' (Ephesians 6:4).

In simple English, this means that they must seek to understand their children and, as they grow up, to remain close to them in thought and sympathy; they must see their point of view and recognise their independence and the right to be independent. As in all other personal relationships there are two sides to it – the parents' and the child's. Each has obligations and responsibilities to the other.

I am sure my answer to Mary must be: 'Try to understand your parents' point of view, listen to their advice and try to see why they are not happy about Michael. Then, when you have given due weight to what they think – and then only – should you come to your decision. If you have to go against their wishes, then do it openly and honestly, trying to make your parents see why you differ from them.'

This is the only way Mary can act with a mature sense of judgement, and the only way she can carry out the Bible teaching of honouring her parents.

The Bible has something to say: see Ephesians 6:1–17.

Christian marriage

Woman 1971

'Till death us do part' is part of the vow taken during a marriage service in the church of England. The words assert the ideal for Christian marriage as a life-long partnership for better or for worse.

To uphold this ideal, the church of England has frowned upon a remarriage of a divorced person in church, and most clergy have refused to take such services. Now at last there is a possibility of an easing of this unhappy situation which has caused so much distress to very sincere people whose first marriage has broken down and who wish to enter their second one with God's blessing.

A Commission has recommended ways and means for making this possible. I only hope the Church will officially adopt these recommendations.

I am glad because for over thirty years I have married in my church people who have previously failed in their first marriage. As a parish priest it was my legal right to do this, even if the official Church disapproved. My view quite simply is that if God forgives sin when we sincerely ask Him, will He not forgive failure in marriage, particularly when divorce was decided on as the lesser of two evils in an unhappy situation? Granted this forgiveness, why cannot the person be remarried with God's blessing if there is a sincere desire to make this second marriage a truly Christian one?

I can't argue all the points out in this short article. But my long experience of following up such second marriages confirms that in very many cases they are tremendously happy and, more important still from my point of view, in many cases the couple thus remarried in church have become or continued to be definite practising Christians, seeking – however imperfectly – to achieve the ideal of Christian marriage.

Each must love his wife as his very self – Ephesians 5:21–33.

Are you a snob?

Woman 1976

It is easy to find this fault in others, difficult to see it in ourselves.

The happy young couple were in my vestry signing the marriage register. To me it had been a specially lovely service, because I knew both of them well. John and Betty had been members of my church and young people's club for several years. They were deeply in love, and were committed Christians.

John had just got a responsible new post, a fascinating one with children, which offered Betty a chance to share in his work. What could be a happier future to which to look forward?

The atmosphere in the vestry was icy. The parents of John stood on one side without a smile or a word of greeting to Betty's parents, standing on the other. There wasn't even a pretence of social appearances to cover up the bitter feelings that John's mother, in particular, felt towards Betty and her family.

And the reason? A sense of social superiority. Betty wasn't good enough for her John. She was of a different class, without their culture.

As I watched sadly, I could not help feeling how often snobbishness spoils personal relationships.

The wealth of our country may be more evenly distributed today than it was. Education is more widely spread, and culture more largely shared. But everywhere there are still the evils of class distinction.

You find it in different canteens in one factory; you find it among neighbours in a street; you find it in differences in schools. People think that other people are not good enough for them.

Obviously, the Bible teaches that not everybody is equally cultured or gifted. We all have different talents, some are more privileged than others. But Jesus did teach quite clearly that God is the Heavenly Father of us all.

He has no favourites, and we have no right to feel superior to anyone else. If we have advantages, then all we should feel is humble gratitude for them.

It is easy to see the fault of snobbishness in other people, but hard to realise when we fall unconsciously into the same temptation ourselves.

One of the best evidences of a truly Christ-like spirit is to be a person free from the attitude of superiority. Instead of looking down on others, we should recognise the fineness in their character and the good points in their personality.

The Bible has something to say: see James 2:1–13.

No one is beyond hope
Woman 1976

Recently, a friend who has been a voluntary prison visitor told me a very interesting thing about men in prison. On the whole, he said, prisoners don't pass judgement on their fellow inmates, no matter what crimes they've committed. But there is an exception to this code: the man who has committed a crime against a child. Almost invariably, such a man becomes afraid to mix with his fellow convicts and, as soon as he can, requests solitary confinement.

The point this illustrates is that even hardened criminals can be touched by the suffering of a child. And if this is so, I feel sure there are other areas where even long-term prisoners can be reached and helped. This is what we mean when we talk about the rehabilitation of prisoners.

An interesting new method of rehabilitation for certain offenders is now being tried. When these men and women, who've been in prison several times, are convicted again, they are put on probation provided they attend a special centre every day. Two probation officers guide the programme, which includes practical subjects like carpentry and a good deal of group discussion, in which they face their individual problems together.

The first few years of this programme have already shown very promising results, with a number of regular criminals being helped to find their real selves and assume responsibility. So you see – no one is beyond hope!

Whoever receives one such child in my name, receives me – Matthew 18:5.

171

Feeling free
Woman 1975

Bert lives in the north of England. He is an emotionally unstable man in his late twenties. As a child he grew up in an unhappy home with a drunken stepfather, and he has never been free of deep suspicion and utter lack of trust in other people.

Bert was sleeping out every night in empty houses and unused huts, and he woke up each morning with an eye on the alert so that he could slip out unnoticed. He felt totally trapped by his circumstances.

Fortunately, a young married couple came to know him and gave him friendship. All they could offer him was the back of their garage to sleep in and washing facilities, but they also gave him their friendship and their trust.

As the months passed, Bert began to regain his trust in other people, he settled down emotionally and gradually began to feel free himself. With this new sense of security his latent artistic gifts began to develop.

Today, there are many people like Bert who are looking for someone to trust in. The crying need is for many more people to show themselves trustworthy and to be the kind of people that others can hold on to when the knocks of life hit them hard.

It's not a bad question to ask oneself: 'Am I the kind of person in whom someone else can place his trust?'

The Giver of the promise may be trusted – Hebrews 10:22.

Integrity as a way of life
Woman 1975

Integrity in daily life is worth a thousand sermons on Christianity and is the reflection of the inner character which others see and take note of.

Recently, I met a man who used to be apprenticed as a jockey in the racing stables at Newmarket and who is now a successful trainer. Although he was doing well, however, he was frustrated and dissatisfied and felt there was something more he ought to do. Then out of the blue he was offered a contract overseas to manage the stable owned by a leading jockey club.

He was told there was a great deal of corruption as well as horse drugging in this particular racing circle, and his job would be to straighten things out.

My friend felt this was the challenge he had been waiting for, and accepted the position. He gradually got rid of the corrupt practices, but found that, largely through ignorance, the grooms were unintentionally being cruel to the horses.

My friend loved and cared for the horses, treating them as individual creatures, and slowly but surely something of his own influence and attitudes began to rub off on the grooms. This situation may seem an unlikely one for influence through Christian integrity and example, but it is striking in that my friend is not a dynamic personality but a straightforward and very humble Christian man. He says what he thinks, and lives what he says. Those with whom he works take note of this quality.

The harvest of the Spirit is goodness, fidelity, gentleness and self-control
— Galatians 5:22–23.

Peace, perfect peace
Woman 1975

Peace is what the world today is longing for. I do not mean simply the ending of wars, but something deeper and more personal.

Some weeks ago the Beatles were at Bangor in North Wales seeking, with the help of an Indian mystic, to find inner quiet and peace of mind.

On the Bank Holiday weekend some thousands of 'flower children' met for a love-in at Woburn Abbey. One of the objects, so they said, was to discover peace and to bring peace to the world.

At the same time, outside my own church in the Bull Ring in the centre of Birmingham, a few young students and teachers fasted for three days and nights in the cause of peace – in their case peace through the end of the Vietnam war.

In a programme on television in the same week I was reminded that some ordinary people in China have never known anything but war for over twenty years.

In all this search for peace what are we really after? It is stating the obvious to say that wars between men and nations ought to cease, for human happiness. But what is our deeper search?

Life is by its very nature a struggle for us on earth – a struggle to survive, a struggle to produce children and to bring them up in the family circle, a struggle to raise standards of living in terms of better health and more material goods. As long as we remain on earth there will always be this element of struggle.

A naturalist once told me that it was only by pushing its way out of the chrysalis that the butterfly got both the strength of its wings and the beauty of its colour. Life in a permanent armchair would not really, if we are honest, be a life worth having.

Yet with the struggle, there can be a peace which all of us need and some of us seriously seek. It is an inner peace with our consciences and in our relationships with others.

It was this peace that Jesus offered to give to His friends. For Him, and in His mind for us too, this inner peace is based on a confidence in God's love and power. The analogy that comes to my mind is the kind of peace that comes to a young man when the girl he loves says she will marry him. The issue is settled and the sense of struggle is over.

Such an inner peace of mind can carry us through the suffering of day by day struggle into a confident and positive kind of living.

Peace I leave with you, my peace I give unto you – John 14:23–31.

Here I stand in the Gospel
by an Evangelist
Tomorrow's Church 1981

Why do I wish to remain anonymous? I hope I do not lack the courage of my convictions. My reason for writing anonymously is that clergymen like myself are apt to judge what they read by what they know of the person who writes it rather than examining the material for its truth or falsity allowing what is written to commend itself or otherwise. About myself I need only say that I have been a priest in the Church of England for forty years or so and for most of that time working as an ordinary parish priest. Perhaps my greatest desire has been to try to communicate the gospel of God's grace to those inside the church and to people outside, always looking to God to lead people into response to his grace.

The stance that I take on the urgency of trying to communicate the gospel, that is to 'evangelise', clearly depends on my doctrinal stance on the gospel itself. So where do I stand?

By the offering of the gospel I mean an offering by life and by word – the life of worship and of everyday behaviour – the word proclaimed publicly or spoken privately. As the gospel is communicated, because I believe it is God's will, I expect that individuals will come into Christian experience which is both similar to and different from, and more complete than, a religious experience. I want people to 'realise their baptism', to come alive to God in Christ, to be reconciled to God in Christ or, to use a doctrinal term, to discover themselves 'justified through grace'. This discovery can happen gradually over a period of time or happen decisively in a crisis conversion.

Such a speaking of the gospel presents a daunting challenge, for as Paul Tillich says: 'There is scarcely any way of making justification through grace intelligible to the modern man. He is so sure of himself, of his knowledge, of his power or the power of the collective.' Yet this is what the gospel is about.

Two corollaries follow from this.

Suffering with Christ in the world

Such reconciliation with God in Christ should inevitably mean that I am prepared to share the fellowship of 'His sufferings', because the God I have discovered is a God of suffering and love. Therefore I must follow Him into his programme for His world. This may mean involvement in the world, in secular life, in politics, *etc.* It will also involve me in the privilege of inviting others to know Christ too because that is the Will of God I have discovered.

Proclaiming to Church people

Because there is a constant tendency in all of us to keep returning to some form of justifying ourselves, the second corollary is that this gospel of justification through Grace needs to be proclaimed plainly to Church people. Christians need to be 'soaked' in this gospel, because there are many in the pews who think they can 'win salvation' and are acceptable to God because of their decent and good lives. This attitude helps to explain the lack of gratitude and joy found in so many church-going people's lives and religion.

Christ and other faiths

I cannot accept the simplistic view that open, devout and spiritual men of other religions, have a relationship with the Living God that is not as real as my own; on the other hand, neither can I accept (as radical theologians suggest) that their relationship with God is just as good as ours and that therefore we have no business to invite them to become Christians.

To me the God of the Bible is a self-disclosing God, ever inviting men into a relationship with Himself and accomplishing this within them when they are open to receive Him. This view of God is focused in the person and the event we call Jesus Christ. Here in Him there is a certainty that God is like that – a reconciling God seeking to bring us to Himself. To discover God in Christ is therefore to come to a fuller understanding of His loving acceptance, the joy of a certainty of a true relationship with Him, and a hope that the reconciliation which is granted to us expresses His purpose for the whole wide world.

In this sense the discovery of God in Christ, and all that that means, is a 'superior' religious experience, though it does not make those who have so discovered God feel superior; rather it humbles us to see ourselves as 'the chief of sinners'. Moreover, the light of God blazing out in Christ is 'inclusive' so that whenever something of this light is seen by those outside the Christian tradition, the Christian rejoices that someone has discovered something of 'Christ incognito'. Indeed we need to recognise that in our every encounter with the living truth of God in Christ, there is always both fulfilment of true insights and longings, and judgement of falsehood and distortion; that holds good for those of other faiths and of none; it also holds good for Christians.

Christ died for us

I am forced by the Scriptures and also by the Sacraments to take seriously the fact that 'Christ died for our sins'. I find it difficult to place any meaning on the idea that Jesus Christ on the Cross is bearing the punishment for my sins at the hands of a just Father in Heaven. I am sure that no one theory of the Atonement can fully express the significance of Calvary as historically it has been experienced by the Christian church. Nevertheless, with all my heart and mind I can say to people: 'Jesus Christ died for you; in His suffering love He faced the consequences of human evil including yours in His death; in Him we see the enigma of the innocent suffering for the guilty, Christ breaking the hold of sin over you. Now you can be certain that the alienation between God and yourself is at an end and that His free and undeserved forgiveness can become the basis of a life lived in ever-deepening dependence on God.'

Crude and simplistic theories of the Atonement do not attract me but the mystery of Christ dying on the Cross and setting us free does hold me. If He had not died, I could not be saved; God by His Resurrection guarantees that I am saved.

The second coming

The fact of 'the End – the Eschaton' – the second coming of Christ – cannot be avoided when we try to communicate the gospel; to me it is an integral part of it, influencing both our words and the way in which we live. I am not particularly interested in details of dates, times, numbers and about the method of Christ's second coming. But I do believe that in Jesus Christ I can discover an inner meaning to history – this is the working out of God's redeeming reconciling purpose for the whole world. In the End He will establish His Kingdom and His purpose will be fulfilled. God will in no respect be defeated. Here is the climax of history. How God's sovereignty will ultimately be established and in which sense the earth will be liberated and transformed I am not clear, but my faith is that human history finds its meaning and its goal in Jesus Christ and all that His Kingdom means. This is my Christian Hope.

Heaven and hell

While I believe that the concepts of heaven and hell express crucial insights into the reality of evil and the reality of being right with God and the reality of human choice, all of which are essential to the preaching of the gospel, I am not happy when these concepts are used to describe the final destiny of individuals. In the end we shall all find ourselves at the mercy of God made plain on the Cross. It is possible for people so to sell themselves to evil as to find themselves in hell, beyond redemption, as we see it but, since in the end redemption is God's act by grace and not in any way my achievement, God can deal even with such people.

Ultimately the victory is the victory of God's love without any defeat. The concept of purgatory may help us here and do justice to much of the severe language of scripture; all of us will face purgatory, if by this we mean a painful yet joyful personal encounter with the love of God; in this encounter we shall know ourselves rightly condemned yet purged by His love so that seeing Him unveiled we shall become like Him as He is.

Authority – three strands

'By what Authority do you assert these points of faith?' A fair question indeed. It sometimes appears that Christians seem apart from each other largely because of the way in which they find the Authority for what they proclaim in the name of Christ. I am not prepared to say my Authority is solely the Scriptures; nor am I happy to say it is solely in the Church.

Christ and the Scriptures

Difficult though it is to put it into words, perhaps I see Authority something like this. From Christ to the Apostles certain insights into God's truths were given not suddenly but gradually. As those first Christians worshipped together, shared their insights, and tried to communicate the gospel, tried to communicate what they knew through Christ to others, their ideas about Jesus Christ became clearer and more articulate. They were convinced that Jesus was truly human, tempted on all points as they had been, yet without sin. They also were convinced that in Him they saw the Father perfect, present and revealed. They could not put down any particular worked-out doctrine of Incarnation, but they treated Jesus Christ as their Lord and their God. They meditated on His atoning death, they meditated His message and His life and, driven by the Spirit, flung themselves into extending His Kingdom.

Gradually over the years the early Christian church put their insights into writing and enshrined them in the Scriptures, recognising in the Old Testament the preparation for the gospel. They also expressed precisely the same insights about Jesus Christ in the two Sacraments they shared – Baptism and the Eucharist. This is the first strand of my Authority.

The Saints

My second strand of Authority is the verification of the experience of the Christ who died for us and who lives in us in the lives of countless Saints who for two thousand years of Christian history have in one way or another borne their witness to the same insights, the same discoveries and the same catholic universal truth.

Inner conviction

The third and final strand is my own inner conviction that came to me when Christ by His Spirit put His grip on me as a young communicant many years ago. I find my Authority not in one or in two but in all three strands together, so that I can speak with a certitude of an inner ring of truth about Jesus Christ and with the hope that I shall one day reach that for which he has taken hold of me.

Just because this kind of Authority is not dogmatically stated in a book of words but is a discovery from experience, there has to be some measure of question and doubt, but we can offer the gospel with conviction speaking out of a 'questioning faith', which at the same time makes clear to our hearers a deep sense of inner conviction. As a matter of fact this openness of attitude draws people from the outside world towards Christ. They want certitude; they don't want slick answers.

The impact of my stance

Why have I inflicted upon you a description of 'my stance in the gospel' in such detail? Firstly, because it has a vital part to play as I try to share the gospel. My certitude of Jesus Christ is part of my life from which I cannot escape nor do I wish to do so. But I cannot speak these words to non-Christians by giving them simply Biblical phrases or some other kind of Christian clichés. As I struggle with the difficult task of communicating the heart of the gospel, through analogies and ideas that will ring a bell to the secularised society of today, I fail and am often frustrated but my stance prevents me losing the gospel in my struggle to communicate.

Secondly my stance gives me an urgency of desire that others may discover the true and deep experience of God in Christ and that in society a true community of living may develop through Him.

Thirdly it gives me a relaxed, not proselytising attitude because I am convinced, frustrated though I may be, but not disheartened.

The pain of being not acceptable

Such a stance in the gospel brings some challenging and often unwelcome consequences. I find that some of my fellow Christians, both clergy and laypeople, are uncomfortable to be partners with me in evangelistic work; sometimes they do not think I am to be trusted to speak the gospel in their churches. This has nothing whatever to do with churchmanship; it has everything to do with my final stance on the gospel.

From my point of view, I am able to work with anybody in communicating the gospel of Christ provided we are sharing the basic gospel of justification through grace. I am more than willing to be open to Christians who in different ways and with different emphases seek to serve this same basic gospel. In fact, I think together we can make a more complete act of sharing.

Yet as I get older and look back, I realise that this stance of mine in the gospel was often unacceptable both to the conservatives on the one side and to the radicals on the other. I was either 'unsound' or of a 'one track mind'. No doubt a good deal of the difficulty lay in my own personality and provocative attitudes but I am sure that a much deeper reason was the question of doctrinal stance.

What we have here is not a division of churchmanship, of ceremonies or of methods. It is in the last analysis a fundamental difference of belief about God's justifying grace and reconciling activity in His world. There is indeed a practical difference between those who are able to include all others who, however, they do it, seek to offer Christ to the people and those who insist that, in addition to offering Christ to the people, He must be offered in a certain rather inflexible way. If we are truly sensitive to God's dealings with men and women, we cannot be bound by any method, nor insist on certain phrases of doctrinal formulations, nor link the gospel with some particular style of Christian living – the gospel and . . . '.

The need for support

Now I come to the reason for making this statement. In coming to the place where I could take 'my stance' I had a pilgrimage that was neither easy nor without pain – the pain of being misunderstood. As my thinking began to develop and as I became more open about it, I realised that I was being misunderstood. I was in fact thrown out of certain circles and was no longer 'in'. I looked for support from other Christians. Was I alone in my thinking – in my changing attitude? The Church indeed was there to hold me. But I needed a closer fellowship, more supportive because we could share with each other, correct and guide each other. I found such a support in a group of friends. But note – their support was not simply that they were questioning and changing and becoming more open; that was important, but far more important was the fact that each and every one of them was seeking to offer the gospel to others and inviting them to become Christians. We were at one not only in our main thinking but in our deeds of evangelising.

I believe that today there are many younger clergymen and younger laymen and woman whose minds are changing, not about the gospel itself, but about the way they think and speak of the gospel. As they become more open where can they turn for support today?

Index of people and places mentioned in
Bryan Green and Peter Grothe's chapters

The Bryan Green Society Ltd
(Registered Charity No 220486)

The Society was established in 1949 by Bryan and Winifred Green to support his work and to assist the development of the liberal evangelical tradition and evangelism worldwide.

This book was produced as a result of the initiative of the Society in recognition of his work, and to ensure that these principles would carry on. Any profit resulting from its sale will be used by the Society to promote the work of evangelism.

Books by Bryan Green:

The Practice of Evangelism (Hodder & Stoughton, 1951)

Being and Believing (Hodder & Stoughton, 1956)

Saints Alive (Epworth Press, 1959)

The Society also holds a quantity of unpublished tapes and sermons. Anyone interested in knowing more should contact: Mrs Gill Bell, Hon Secretary, The Bryan Green Society Ltd, 68 Southern Road, Thame, Oxon OX9 2DZ